Sprachwelten Englisch

Highland Heroes

Kirsten Marsh
Jennifer Muir
Sarah Trenker

compact

Baierbrunner Straße 27, 81379 München
Ausgabe 2018

Redaktion: Sigrid Schulz
Fachkorrektur: Nathalie Russell
Produktion: Ute Hausleiter
Titelillustration: shutterstock.com/Olga_Angelloz
Gestaltung: red.sign GbR, Stuttgart
Umschlaggestaltung: red.sign GbR, Stuttgart

ISBN 978-3-8174-1936-4
381741936/1

www.compactverlag.de

Lesen und Lernen mit den Sprachwelten

So abwechslungsreich war Englischlernen noch nie! Die Sprachwelten kombinieren unterhaltsames Lesen mit dem bewährten didaktischen Konzept der Reihe Lernkrimi. Die vier Kurzgeschichten sind von **muttersprachlichen Autoren** verfasst und genau auf Ihr **Lernniveau** abgestimmt – perfekt für den Unterricht oder ganz individuelles Lernen.

Wörter, die noch unbekannt sind, werden direkt auf der Seite übersetzt, so ist kein zusätzliches Nachschlagen erforderlich. Das **alphabetische Glossar** am Ende des Buches bietet eine Übersicht aller **Vokabeln** mit ihren Übersetzungen. Im **Phase6-Vokabeltrainer** sind diese sogar vertont.

Jede Kurzgeschichte enthält abwechslungsreiche, auf den Text bezogene **Übungen** zu Wortschatz, Grammatik und Textverständnis, die zum aktiven Lernen motivieren. Überprüfen Sie Ihren Lernerfolg einfach im **Abschlusstest**. Im Anhang finden Sie alle **Lösungen**.

Ergänzend zu jeder Kurzgeschichte verweisen **Infokästen** auf sprachliche und landeskundliche Besonderheiten.

Inhalt

Till Death Us Do Part

Sarah Trenker

Charles und Rosemary Waters führen seit über 40 Jahren eine Ehe mit klassischer Rollenverteilung. Seitdem der ehemalige Geschäftsführer Charles in Rente ist, fokussiert sich sein ausgeprägtes Kontrollbedürfnis jedoch zunehmend auf seine Frau Rosemary. Mit großer Geduld erträgt sie seine Launen, solange ihr auch Auszeiten mit ihren Freundinnen vergönnt sind. Als Charles ihr diese Freude jedoch auch noch nehmen möchte, trifft sie eine Entscheidung ...

Charles Waters, ehemaliger Geschäftsführer eines großen Konzerns, ist mittlerweile im Ruhestand – zum Segen seiner Mitarbeiter und zum Leidwesen seiner Frau. Er ist selbstherrlich, stur und egoistisch und liebt es, andere herumzukommandieren.

Rosemary Waters ist liebenswert, geduldig und die perfekte Ehefrau und Mutter. Für sie bedeutet Ehe „bis dass der Tod uns scheidet".

Christine Cole ist Rosemarys beste Freundin. Sie ist geschieden und eine unabhängige, glückliche Frau.

"Rosemary!"
"Yes, **dear**."
"Come here!"
"What do you want, dear?"
"Where is my blue shirt?"
"It's on the door."
"Which door?"
"The bedroom door, dear!
"And my **tie**?"
Rosemary is standing in the **hall** looking up towards the bedroom. "You're only taking the car to the **garage**, darling!"
Charles comes to the top of the stairs. His face is very red. Rosemary knows what is coming.
"I want to wear a tie to the garage. I am going to wear a tie to the garage. I don't want them thinking that they can do bad work because I am no longer **head** of a big company. You don't understand such things. You never worked. Now, just tell me where my blue tie is!"
"It's on the door in the **wardrobe**," Rosemary answers. She does not say, "where all your ties are", because Charles doesn't have a **sense of humour**.
"Do you want a cup of tea before you go?"
"No! I want a coffee."
"But you know what the **GP** says."
"Get me a coffee, woman! How does the doctor know what I need for breakfast?"

dear	Liebster, Schatz
tie	Krawatte
hall	*hier:* Diele
garage	*hier:* Werkstatt
head	*hier:* Geschäftsführer, Chef
wardrobe	Kleiderschrank
sense of humour	Sinn für Humor
GP	Hausarzt

Um im Englischen auszudrücken, dass es viel von etwas gibt, verwendet man **many** für zählbare (dogs, books) oder **much** für nicht zählbare (water, love) Begriffe. Falls man unsicher ist, kann man auch **lots of** bzw. **a lot of** mit allen Substantiven – zählbar und unzählbar – benutzen!

Rosemary **sighs** and walks back into the kitchen to make her husband a cup of coffee. Charles has high **blood pressure**, which is why their GP tells her not to give him too much[i] coffee or butter or too many steaks or desserts. She works hard to make him things that are good for him.

But Charles is Charles, and if he doesn't want to do something, even if it's good for him, then he doesn't do it. Rosemary puts some coffee in the cup. She can hear Charles talking to himself in the bedroom. He **is in a bad mood**. And it is such a nice day. Rosemary looks out of the kitchen window into the garden. It is so beautiful. She smiles. She loves this time of year and working in the garden. Now that Charles is **retired**, Rosemary works out in the garden a lot.

Exercise 1: Much or many? Unterstreichen Sie die richtige Variante!

1. How *much* / many money do you have?
2. Charles Waters has much / many different ties.
3. It doesn't take much / many minutes to get to the garage.
4. Charles doesn't have much / many time for GPs.
5. How much / many times a year do you take the car to the garage?

She hears Charles coming down the stairs and puts his coffee on the table. Her husband walks into the kitchen and sits down. He looks at the newspaper on the table, puts some milk into his cup and drinks. Then he looks at Rosemary:

to sigh	seufzen
blood pressure	Blutdruck
to be in a bad mood	schlecht gelaunt sein
retired	in Rente
health	Gesundheit
moustache	Schnurrbart
to twitch	zucken

"This coffee is like water, Rosemary!"
"Yes, dear. Dr Arkwright says…"
"I don't care what Dr Arkwright says."
"I know, but I do. And because he says it is important for your **health**…"
Charles's[i] face is red again and his **moustache** is **twitching** – which is never good.
"Dr Arkwright is not your husband, I am. And when I ask for a coffee, just do what I ask, PLEASE! And no, I don't want pasta for lunch again. I want a steak!"

> Im Englischen wird das Genitiv **-s** immer mit einem Apostroph angehängt, z.B. **Rosemary's husband** (der Mann von Rosemary). Das ist auch der Fall bei Namen, die auf „s" enden, z.B. **Charles's face.**

Rosemary smiles. "Today I'm having lunch with Christine at 11 and I won't be back until 3 p.m. I'm sure you can get a steak in town. And there is a cheese quiche and some salad in the fridge."
"Then make me steak for dinner, woman!" Charles storms out of the kitchen. Rosemary sits down at the kitchen table.

"Why do you make life so difficult for us?" she asks the empty chair. "Life could be so good now that you are retired."

The chair doesn't say anything, so Rosemary stands up and puts her husband's cup and **saucer** into the **dishwasher**, as she does every day. Life is more difficult now that Charles is at home all the time.

Exercise 2: In the house. **Welche Wörter passen zusammen? Ordnen Sie zu!**

1. ☐ cup	a) wardrobe
2. ☐ milk	b) table
3. ☐ shirt	c) fridge
4. ☐ chair	d) pressure
5. ☐ blood	e) saucer

Rosemary can't **remember** when she stopped loving Charles, but it was before the children started school. For him, everything was always about work. And he was only nice to their children, Henry and Samantha, when they did well at school. And at 65, Rosemary thinks, he is no better with his grandchildren. They run to their bedrooms **as soon as** they come to visit. Charles does not know how to speak to children. He asks them about their work and where they want to be in a few years' time.
Last time he did this, Henry, who is **usually** very **patient** with his father, got very angry. "Father!! John is seven years old. Do you really think he knows

saucer	Untertasse
dishwasher	Geschirrspüler
to remember	sich erinnern
as soon as	sobald
usually	normalerweise
patient	geduldig

what he wants to do when he is twenty?"
"I did," answered Charles, his moustache twitching.
The phone rings.
"569123." i
"Morning Rosemary, it's Christine."
"Hello Christine. Are we still meeting at 11? Please don't tell me you can't."

of course	natürlich, gewiss
↯ **Thank goodness!**	Gott sei Dank!
to enjoy oneself	Spaß haben
to imagine	sich vorstellen

"Oh dear, is Charles in a good mood again?"
"You know Charles," Rosemary sighs.
"Yes, we all do. But no, 11 is the right time. Bring a swimming costume with you. The weather is so good. Perhaps we can go for a swim in the river? What do you think?"
"Wonderful idea!"
As soon as Rosemary puts the phone down, it rings again.
"56…"
"Mum, it's me!"
"Samantha? Are you okay? Are you phoning from work?"
"No, Mum. We're in Devon. Do you remember?"
Rosemary laughs. "Sorry, darling. Yes, **OF COURSE** I remember. Your mother never forgets things, as you know."
Now Samantha laughs. "**Thank goodness** for that!"
"Are you having a good time? Is the hotel nice? Are the children **enjoying themselves**?" asks Rosemary.
"Yes, yes, and yes," Samantha replies. Rosemary **imagines** her daughter sitting on the beach watching her children playing with her husband Nicholas.

i In Großbritannien war es früher normal sich mit der Telefonnummer zu melden. Heutzutage hört man das, wenn überhaupt, eher nur noch bei älteren Menschen. Die meisten Leute sagen einfach, „Hello" oder „Hello, NAME speaking."

"How are things with you, Mum?"
"The same **as usual**. I'm going out with Christine today."
"That's good. But why don't you **go away** for a week?"
"You know your father doesn't like holidays, Samantha."
"You could go **on your own**. Or come and stay with us."
Rosemary laughs. "No, I'm fine. Your father needs me here."
"Hmm..."
Rosemary knows what her daughter is thinking. "Come on Samantha, he's not THAT bad."
"Oh mother, yes he is! You know he is. And he's **getting worse** all the time."
Rosemary laughs. "That's enough Samantha. He's your father. You enjoy your holiday and don't think about me. I'm fine. I love you."
"I love you, too, Mum."

Exercise 3: Verb forms. Lesen Sie weiter und setzen Sie die Verben in der richtigen Form ein!

lose | look | find | ~~ring~~ | be | take | forget | tell

When she puts the phone down it **1.** *rings* again.

"Hello... Samantha? Did you **2.** ______________ something?"

"Yes, Mum. I forgot to **3.** ______________ you that I found the money I **4.** ______________ last week."

"That's great dear. Where **5.** ______________ it?

"In the sports bag I **6.** ______________ to the swimming pool."

"That's great, darling."

"**7.** ______________ after yourself, Mum..."

"Samantha, I **8.** ____________ a big girl. I can look after myself!"

Christine and Rosemary do not get back from lunch until 3.30 p.m. They sit in the car in front of the house for a few minutes.

as usual	wie üblich
to go away	*hier:* verreisen
on one's own	allein
to get worse	schlimmer werden
lovely	schön
to giggle	kichern
suddenly	plötzlich
serious	ernst
sparkling	glitzernd, funkelnd
to marry	heiraten

"Thank you so much Christine. That was a **lovely** afternoon."

Christine sighs. "You do know he is watching us from the kitchen. Please take one of my cigarettes and put it in your mouth."

Rosemary **giggles**. "Oh Christine, my life is difficult enough as it is."

Her friend is **suddenly serious**. "You know, you could come to us if you ever want to ..."

"I'm fine."

Christine smiles again. "Yes, you're always fine Rosemary. And you do look good now after four hours away from your husband... Your green eyes are **sparkling**. As I said, ..."

"Yes, yes," answers Rosemary as she gets out of the car with a smile. "As I said, I'm fine."

Rosemary can never forget that Charles is the father of her two wonderful children. He was very different when they first met. She loved him a lot when they **married**. It is very different now, but she is also not the same young woman. And she **promised** at her **wedding**, "**Till death us do part**", and that is a promise for life.

Exercise 4: Spot the mistakes. Welcher Satz ist fehlerfrei? Kreuzen Sie an!

1. ❒ **a)** He has a bad mood.
   ❒ **b)** He is in a bad mood.

2. ❒ **a)** Christine and I are going out for lunch.
   ❒ **b)** Me and Christine are going out for lunch.

3. ❒ **a)** Christine is seriously.
   ❒ **b)** Christine is serious.

4. ❒ **a)** She gives him the coffee.
   ❒ **b)** She gives to him the coffee.

5. ❒ **a)** He is the children's father.
   ❒ **b)** He is the childrens' father.

to promise	versprechen
wedding	Hochzeit
ϟ Till death us do part	Bis dass der Tod uns scheidet
in public	in der Öffentlichkeit

When she walks through the door Charles is waiting for her. His face is very red again.
"Hello, dear."
"Do you know what time it is?"
"Christine and I went swimming because the weather was so nice. We forgot the time."
"You FORGOT the time! And MY tea!" Charles puts his face very close to Rosemary's. "Aren't you two a bit too old to go swimming **in public**? It isn't very nice for other people!"

"Perhaps I am just too old to **care**," she replies. Then before Charles can say anything, "I'll get you some tea and **biscuits**. Were you **successful** with the car?"
"Of course I was successful with the car! Bring the tea to my **study**. I need you to write a letter for me."
"Yes, dear."
"And I hope you got some steak for me."
"I did, dear."
"I like it **rare**."
"I know."

to care	sich kümmern, Gedanken machen
biscuit	Keks
successful	erfolgreich
study	*hier:* Arbeitszimmer
rare	*hier:* blutig
to look after sb./sth.	für jmd. / etw. sorgen
Old Staff Association	Verband ehem. Mitarbeiter
wife	Ehefrau
to humiliate	erniedrigen

For a while, life goes on in the same way, and Rosemary is happy enough. She **looks after** Charles and tries to keep him happy, too. She has the garden, her children and her friends and theatre evenings. Charles has his club, his study and the **Old Staff Association**.
Rosemary doesn't like the men at the club because they are all very like Charles. And so she is happy that it is a men's club. But sometimes Charles makes her go with him to the Old Staff Association lunches and dinners – which he loves, of course. He is the old boss and feels like a king. But he often says things there to make Rosemary feel bad.
"My **wife** can't understand a lot of the things we are talking about... She left school at sixteen and just worked in a shop in Hastings... She lived with her parents until I married her... She was lucky to get me..." And so on. Rosemary always feels **humiliated**.

Exercise 5: Translation match-up. **Wie lautet die richtige Übersetzung? Ordnen Sie zu!**

1. ☐ lovely	a) schlimmer
2. ☐ worse	b) erfolgreich
3. ☐ public	c) ernst
4. ☐ successful	d) schön
5. ☐ serious	e) Öffentlichkeit

As long as Rosemary can get away to the theatre or for lunch with Christine, everything is fine. But then things begin to change.

Rosemary is now the only person Charles can control. His **employees** at the company were happy to see him go and never contact him. No one from the **company** ever calls him. No one wants his help and no one misses him.

At the Old Staff Association meetings, he sits together with all the other managers who never get any phone calls. Rosemary often sits at another table. Charles thinks that this is so he and the "boys" can talk together about the old days. Rosemary knows it is so she and the other employees and ex-employees can have some fun without them.

employee	Angestellte/r
company	Firma
HR (Human Resources)	Personal-abteilung

Matthew, Charles's **HR** manager for many years, often says with a smile, "They can talk about the good old days for ever!" He and Rosemary often sit together. She knows from him that everyone is **thankful** to the old managers for making the company successful. But they are also thankful that they are now retired. Rosemary knows from many of the old employees that Charles was not a nice manager. When he was a manager, people who didn't want to do everything as he wanted soon left the company.

thankful	dankbar
instead	stattdessen
to manage	regeln, leiten
tasty	schmackhaft, lecker

Charles likes controlling people. While he was working, it was not a big problem for Rosemary. She was free to do what she wanted during the day. Now Charles is at home all the time. He no longer plays golf, and he doesn't have any hobbies at home. **Instead**, he tries to **manage** everything Rosemary does in the house. He even goes shopping with her to make sure she always buys the cheapest products. Not that money is a problem. Charles has a good pension(i). But having total control makes Charles feel good.

Rosemary patiently did what Charles wanted for a very long time. Then one day, it was a Tuesday, she could be patient no longer. On this day she made Charles a cheese omelette for breakfast. Low fat cheese but still very **tasty**.

"Rosemary!"

"Yes, dear."

"I don't want you to go out with Christine today."

Rosemary puts the butter back in the fridge.

"But why, Charles? You know Christine is my best friend."

"And you know that I don't like her."

"But why?"

"She is not good for you."

False friends!
pension ≠ Pension
pension = Rente
rent = Miete

"What do you mean?"
"Because of her, you ask too many questions."
"You always told the children that asking questions was good."
Although I do remember that you didn't like it when your daughter asked too many questions, Rosemary thinks to herself.
Charles starts eating his omelette and answers with his mouth full of food. He knows that Rosemary hates it when he does that.
"Yes, dear. But I think the questions Christine puts in your head are not good for us."
"Not good for *us*, Charles – or not good for *you*? And which questions, anyway? I am not sure I know what you mean."
Charles stops eating. His moustache is twitching. "She is changing you. You're **becoming** too **independent**."

although	obwohl
to become	werden
independent	unabhängig
upset	aufgebracht, verärgert
suffocating	erstickend

"What?! I still do all the work of a 1950s wife, don't I?"
Rosemary is beginning to get really **upset**. She does everything for Charles. But it is so difficult with him now that he is at home all the time. She finds Charles **suffocating**, and so she also needs time for herself. Now he wants to take those few hours away as well.
Charles is smiling now, happy that his wife is upset.
"I don't understand you sometimes, Charles. You know it isn't good for us to spend every minute of the day together. But last week you stopped me from going to the cinema with the girls from the tennis club. On Monday you suddenly needed the car so I couldn't go swimming with Fiona. And this is the second time you want to stop me from going out with Christine.

Why? They are the only things in the week that I do without you. What's wrong with you?"

Exercise 6: Pronouns. Ersetzen Sie die fett gedruckten Wörter durch Pronomen!

1. You know **Christine** is **Rosemary's** best friend.

   *You know **she** is **her** best friend.*

2. **Charles** starts eating **the omelette**.

   ____

3. **Charles and Rosemary** talk about **the girls**.

   ____

4. **Christine and I** are going to a restaurant.

   ____

5. I hope **the waiter** gives **Christine and me** a good table.

   ____

"What's wrong with me?" Charles is not smiling now. His face is dark red and he stands up. "I am **sick of** you listening to other people but not to me. Dr Arkwright tells you to give me low-fat food, and I tell you that I don't want it. Who do you listen to? Dr Arkwright. Your girlfriends tell you that they go on biking or walking holidays with their husbands, and suddenly you want me to do the same. And where did you get the idea about the spa hotel in Bath?

to be sick of sth. etw. satt haben

Rosemary looks at her husband and her **expression** changes. "And you don't like me **worrying** about your health. Is that what you are saying?"

"I am saying that I know what is best for me. I don't need you listening to everyone else instead of me."

"Okay, dear. If that is what you want, then that is what you'll get."

Charles smiles, but it is not a nice smile. "That sounds better. Now get me some bacon and eggs. I don't want this omelette!"

expression	Ausdruck
to worry	sich Sorgen machen
to order about	herumkommandieren
to send shivers up and down sb.'s spine	jmd. einen Schauder über den Rücken jagen
surprised	überrascht

"Yes, dear."

Later on, when Charles goes to his study to read the newspaper, Rosemary phones Christine to tell her that she cannot get away. Her friend is not happy, but she knows Charles and how difficult it is for Rosemary.

"How long are you going to let him **order you about** like an employee?"

"From today, for as long as it takes."

There is something in Rosemary's voice that sends **shivers up and down** Christine's **spine**.

Christine and Rosemary don't see each other for the next five weeks. When they meet, Christine is **surprised**. Rosemary looks wonderful.

It is a Wednesday, and Rosemary phones to say that Charles is at the doctor's. She has two hours to wait. Does Christine have time for a coffee?

Christine laughs. "Time? Of course I've got time[i] for a coffee with you!! I'll be there in 15 minutes."

Exercise 7: Negatives. Verneinen Sie die folgenden Sätze.

1. Charles wants Rosemary to listen to other people.

Charles doesn't want Rosemary to listen to other people.

2. He is happy about the spa hotel in Bath.

____

3. She can understand why he is upset.

____

4. I am going to let him order me about.

____

5. I need time for myself.

____

Christine walks over to Rosemary's table. "You look great. You're wearing makeup again – and that dress is very sexy. Have you got a new lover?!"

Rosemary smiles. "No, I'm just feeling good."

Wendungen mit time

to have (got) time	Zeit haben
all the time	die ganze Zeit
a long time ago	vor langer Zeit
to spend time	Zeit verbringen
waste of time	Zeitverschwendung

"And Charles is being nice to you...?"

"No. But it is easier now, because I am doing everything that Charles wants me to do."

"But you always do that, don't you?"

"No, in the past I often tried to make him do things that the doctor thought he should do. I cooked him things that he didn't want to eat. I tried to get him to go outside and not drink too much alcohol."

"And now you don't...?"

Rosemary looks up and into the eyes of her best friend. "No, Christine, now I don't. It makes life much easier."

"Oh!"

Christine is not sure what to say. Rosemary looks at her friend and smiles again. It is a smile that Christine doesn't recognize. But then she does, it is a... **selfish** smile. Her friend is thinking about herself. Christine's eyes **twinkle**. "Well, I think it is just right for you and Charles. How about a glass of wine?"

Her best friend giggles – a wonderful **carefree** giggle that makes Christine laugh, too.

"Why not? I can have one glass. But not more because I am driving Charles home."

"So he lets you drive these days? I thought he didn't like women driving?" Christine grins.

"He finds it more **comfortable**."

"Comfortable?!"

"Why don't you come to tea next Sunday. The kids are coming as well."

"Samantha and Henry are visiting Charles...? And I can come as well..."

"Rosemary grins. "Yes, you must come and see for yourself."

"I'll be there!" Christine laughs.

selfish	selbstsüchtig, egoistisch
to twinkle	zwinkern, funkeln
How about...?	Wie wäre es mit ...?
carefree	sorglos
comfortable	bequem
almost ready	fast fertig
chat	Gespräch, Plausch
habits *pl*	Angewohnheiten
to growl	knurren

Exercise 8: Reflexive pronouns. Vervollständigen Sie die Sätze mit den fehlenden Reflexivpronomen!

1. Rosemary drives the car *herself*.

2. Henry wants to see the house for ________________.

3. I chose the dress ________________.

4. Why don't you come and have a look for ________________?

5. The children were old enough to dress ________________.

At 3.30 p.m. Rosemary goes to get Charles from the doctor's. Charles looks unhappy. Rosemary looks at Dr Arkwright. He doesn't look very happy either[i].

"Good afternoon, Mrs Waters. We're **almost ready**. Your husband still needs to do one more thing. Perhaps we could have a little **chat** while nurse Morris looks at his blood pressure."

"Don't you let Dr Arkwright talk to you about bad **habits** again, Rosemary," **growls** Charles.

"No, dear, don't worry," says Rosemary, and she smiles at Dr Arkwright.

Charles goes off with the nurse and Rosemary goes with Dr Arkwright.

"Please sit down, Mrs Waters. How are you? I must say you look very fit."

Rosemary sits down. "I feel very fit, Dr Arkwright."

She looks at the doctor. They know each other well.

> Um zu sagen, dass jemand etw. macht wie jemand anderes, sagt man z.B. „He looks happy, **too**." (Er sieht auch glücklich aus.)
> In Verneinungssätzen verwendet man „either":
> „He doesn't look happy, **either**."
> (Er sieht auch nicht glücklich aus.)

"What does your husband mean when he says 'bad habits'?"
"He does not want me to worry about what he eats or tell him about all the things that are good for his health."
"So?"
"So, Dr Arkwright, I stopped worrying about them, because I can't change my husband – and if he doesn't want to change his habits, then they are not going to change, are they?"
Rosemary looks up at the doctor. What will he think of her? She is surprised to see his expression. There is a little smile in his eyes.

glad	froh
the impossible	das Unmögliche
pill	Tablette
to remind sb. to do sth.	jmd. daran erinnern, etw. zu tun
It's up to you	*hier:* Es liegt ganz an Ihnen

"I think your husband is old enough to know what is good for him and what is not good for him. I am also **glad** to see that you are no longer trying to do **the impossible**."
The nurse walks back into the room with Charles, who stands at the door and growls at Rosemary again. "It's time to go, Rosemary. Don't keep Dr Arkwright chatting. He has important things to do."
Dr Arkwright stands up and holds out his hand to Rosemary. "It is always lovely to see you Mrs Waters. I'd like to see your husband again in six weeks. Please remember to go and get the new **pills**. And please **remind** your husband to take them."
Looking at Charles, he says, "And Mr Waters, of course **it's up to you** what you do."
When Christine arrives at the house the next Sunday, Henry and Samantha are already there with their families. The children are in the garden playing. Samantha opens the door.

Exercise 9: Remember or remind? Unterstreichen Sie die richtige Variante!

1. Dr Arkwright reminds / remembers Charles to take his pills.
2. Charles reminds / remembers to go and get the pills.
3. Rosemary finds it difficult to remind / remember telephone numbers.
4. Charles doesn't like it when the doctor reminds / remembers him to take his pills.
5. Please remind / remember me to phone the garage about the car.

"Hello, Christine. How lovely to see you after such a long time. How are you?"
"Very well. How are you? It is nice... to find you all here..."
The house is full of the **smell** of freshly baked cakes. Christine goes with Samantha into the kitchen where she finds Rosemary with her son Henry and his wife Susan. They are laughing about something with Rosemary.
"Christine is here," says Samantha. They all come over to say hello. Christine sees **at least** six cakes on the table behind them. "**Good heavens**! How many people are coming to tea?"
Samantha looks at her mother. "Father likes his cakes, doesn't he Mum?"

smell	*hier:* Duft
at least	mindestens, zumindest
⚡ **Good heavens!**	Um Himmels Willen!

"Yes, darling. He does."
Christine looks round "And where is Charles?"
"He's in the study with Roger."
Samantha laughs. "Yes, Roger is talking about important business with our father. The Diesel scandal or something."
Christine giggles. "I see."
"Let's take the cakes into the **dining room**. Charles and Roger will be coming soon."
Why is everyone smiling? Christine asks herself. She walks into the dining room with one of the cakes.
"Why are there only two **plates** on the table? Should I get some more?"

probably	wahrscheinlich
dining room	Esszimmer
plate	Teller
to explain	erklären
to take turns	sich abwechseln
to choose	wählen
to shuffle	schlurfen
obese	fettleibig

"Oh, we don't have tea with my father," Henry **explains**. Roger and I **take turns** chatting to my father about something. It keeps him happy and gives my mother a chance to play with her grandchildren and chat to us. We all sit outside in the garden when the weather is good, or in the kitchen when it's raining."
"Yes," says Samantha. "We put all the cakes on the table here first. Dad **chooses** the cakes he wants, then we take the others outside."
A door opens in the house and Christine hears two men speaking. They walk very slowly towards the dining room door. Roger walks through the door first, followed by Charles. But Charles doesn't walk through the door, he **shuffles** through it. He was always fat, but now he is **obese**. His eyes are on the cakes on the table.
He shuffles over to the table and sits down. Then he looks up

at everybody. His face is like a big red **plum** with two little eyes and a moustache. His mouth opens and closes all the time like a fish out of water.

"Hello, Christine. **Long time no see**," he says. "I saw your ex-husband at the club last week, though. He looks very well and seems very happy with Fiona."

"Yes, they are made for each other," Christine smiles. "I also enjoy the extra space in our house. And I have much less work without a man around – far fewer (i) cakes to bake."

plum	Pflaume
Long time no see!	Lange nicht gesehen!
to continue	fortfahren
The way to a man's heart is through his stomach.	Liebe geht durch den Magen.

Somebody – perhaps it is Fiona, Christine is not sure – giggles. Charles's face, if it is possible, goes an even deeper red.

"Hmm. There are wives that enjoy baking for their husbands. Rosemary bakes the most wonderful cakes for me. And Samantha and Fiona bring me cakes, too. They know what a woman's role is."

"Yes, and I'm sure they are both perfect 1950s wives," Christine laughs.

> **Less** und **fewer** bedeuten beide „weniger". Der Unterschied (wie bei „much" und „many") hängt davon ab, ob die Nomen zählbar (fewer) oder unzählbar (less) sind. Daher heißt es z.B. „**less** work, time, money, information", aber "**fewer** cakes, cars, telephones, employees".

"Hmm," Charles growls.

"But yes," she **continues**, every man likes a wife who can cook. As they say: '**The way to a man's heart is through his stomach.**' Of course, some women make millions of cakes and still don't find the heart..."

She stops when she sees Rosemary looking at her. Rosemary

smiles. "Christine just wanted to say hello, Charles, before we sit outside in the garden together. I know you want to talk to Roger about the project in France. It sounds very interesting – at least, what I can understand of it."

sweetly	süß
greedily	gierig
gateau	Torte
lemon curd tart	Zitronentorte
priceless	unbezahlbar
to aim at sth.	auf etw. (ab)zielen

"Which isn't much, I'm sure," says Charles.
"So, darling, which of these cakes would you like to try?" Rosemary continues **sweetly**.
Charles looks **greedily** at the cakes on the table. "I'll take the chocolate **gateau**, the cheesecake, the **lemon curd tart** and the strawberry cream cake."
Out in the garden, Samantha starts laughing. "The way to a man's heart is through his stomach. Although some people still don't find... Christine, you are **priceless**."
Christine smiles and then looks at Rosemary, her expression suddenly serious. "Sorry, Rosemary . I didn't want to upset you."
Rosemary's eyes twinkle. "Don't worry, Christine. You are actually right. I am ***aiming*** at his heart. With cake. More tea, anyone?

Highland Heroes

Jennifer Muir

Morag McKay lebt mit ihrem Vater auf einer abgelegenen Farm in den schottischen Highlands. Es ist ein bescheidenes, aber glückliches Leben. Eines Tages bekommen sie unerwarteten Besuch. Es gilt ein Leben zu retten ...

Morag McKay ist zwölf Jahre alt und ein ungestümes, wildes Mädchen. Sie liebt Tiere und die Natur.

Mr McKay ist Farmer und Morags Vater. Er hat ein hartes, schroffes Äußeres, aber darunter verbirgt sich ein weicher Kern.

Sergeant Campbell ist der Bezirkspolizist des Dorfes.

Morag puts the last of the dinner plates in the **sink** and turns on the hot water. She listens to the wind and rain in the darkness outside.

"I hope Dad isn't much longer", she thinks.

Spring is a hard time on their farm in the highlands[i] of Scotland. The weather can still be very cold and wet. But lots of new lambs are born and Morag's dad often has to look after the sheep until very late at night.

Suddenly there is a **strange** sound. Morag turns off the water to listen. There it is again! A scratching sound at the door.

"Dad?' she calls, "Is that you?"

There is no answer. Nervously Morag walks across the kitchen and opens the heavy wooden door.

"Well, where did you come from?" **exclaims** Morag.

Her **surprise visitor** is a small black and white dog. The dog is very dirty and **shaking** with cold. **Carefully** she picks it up and carries it inside.

"Sssh," **whispers** Morag as she wraps the dog in a warm **towel**. "You're okay now. I've got you."

She sits down in the chair by the fire, holding the dog in her arms. Slowly the dog stops shaking.

Suddenly the farmhouse door bangs open and Mr Mc-Kay walks in. As he shakes

sink	Spülbecken
strange	seltsam, merkwürdig
to exclaim	ausrufen
surprise visitor	Überraschungsbesuch
to shake	beben, zittern
carefully	vorsichtig
to whisper	flüstern
towel	Handtuch

Das schottische Hochland liegt im nordwestlichen Teil Schottlands. Es besteht aus gebirgigen Gegenden sowie großen baumlosen Mooren. Die weitläufige Region mit ihren kargen Bergen und Seen ist wohl das, was viele vor Augen haben, wenn sie an Schottland denken.

the raindrops from his thick, black beard, Mr McKay looks at his daughter sitting by the fire. She is completely focused on something on her knees. He can't see what it is because her long, **ginger** hair is **covering** it and her face.

"What have you got there my love?" he asks.

"Oh Dad," replies Morag. "Look at this poor wee[i] thing. I just found him at the door. I think he's **lost**."

Mr McKay **kneels** by his daughter's chair and **gently examines** the dog.

ginger	*hier:* rothaarig
to cover	bedecken, abdecken
to be lost	*hier:* sich verlaufen haben
to kneel	knien
gently	sanft, behutsam
to examine	untersuchen
collar	*hier:* Halsband
to stroke	streicheln
to whimper	wimmern, winseln
to seem	scheinen, wirken
worried	besorgt
blanket	Decke
cheek	Wange
mat	(Fuß-)Matte

"Well, he's definitely someone's pet," says Mr McKay looking at the **collar** around the dog's neck. "It says his name is Dougal. There are no contact details for the owner."

"Hello Dougal," says Morag, **stroking** his soft ears.

When he hears his name, Dougal suddenly comes out from under the towel and jumps to the floor. He goes over to the door and **whimpers**.

Schottisches Englisch (Standard Scottish English bzw. Scots) hat zahlreiche sprachliche Besonderheiten: Z.B. "wee" bedeutet ‚little' (klein): „I'll have a wee bit more". Sehr oft hört man auch „aye" (klingt wie ‚eye') für ‚yes'.

"What's wrong with him Dad?" asks Morag.

"I'm not sure. He **seems** to be very tired. He must have walked a long way across the hills. But he also seems **worried** about something."

Dougal scratches at the door and whimpers again.
"You can't go out there again tonight," says Mr McKay, picking up the small dog in his big hands. "It's too cold and wet - and dark. You would get lost. You must stay with us tonight. We will try to find your owner in the morning."

That night, Morag cannot sleep. Perhaps it is because of the storm outside, she thinks. But as she lies awake in her bed, she can hear Dougal in the kitchen. When Morag and her father went to bed, they put a **blanket** and some water by the fire for him, but Dougal is not sleeping. Morag can hear him walking round the kitchen, scratching at the door and whimpering. As she falls back to sleep, Morag thinks how sad the little dog sounds.

Exercise 1: Fill in the blanks. Lesen Sie weiter und setzen Sie die angegebenen Wörter richtig ein!

visitor | tired | kisses | rest | porridge

Mr McKay is in the kitchen making **1.** ____________ when Morag comes downstairs in the morning. She walks over to him and **2.** ____________ his **cheek**.
"How is our little **3.** ____________ this morning?" she asks.
"See for yourself."
Dougal is asleep on the **mat** right in front of the door.
"Poor wee dog," says Mr McKay. "He's so **4.** ____________.
I don't think he slept a minute all night. We'll let him have a **5.** ____________ this morning and then we should think about how to find his owner. Maybe we should hang up some posters."

After breakfast, Morag rides her bicycle to the next village to buy fresh bread rolls for lunch. She and her Dad have the same routine every Saturday. After a busy morning on the farm they sit down together for a lunch of soup and sandwiches. Morag puts her bicycle against the window of the bakery and goes inside. The bakery is busy this morning so Morag has to wait in a **queue**. There are two old ladies talking in front of Morag.

queue	(Warte-)Schlange
hiker	Wanderer
Mountain Rescue Team	Bergrettung
counter	Theke, Tresen
to decide	sich entscheiden
to sigh	seufzen

"... have you heard about the missing **hiker**, Edith?" asks the smaller of the two ladies, Mrs Ross. Morag knows her from church.

"No, what do you mean?"

"Well, it was on the radio this morning," replies Mrs Ross. "A man from the next town went walking in the hills yesterday. He never came home. His wife is really worried. She rang the police when it began to get dark. The **Mountain Rescue Team** has been out all night looking for him."

"That's terrible," says Edith. "Do they know what has happened to him?"

Morag tries to see what is happening at the end of queue. The lady at the **counter** is taking a long time **deciding** what to buy.

"... Maybe he has fallen and hurt himself," continues Mrs Ross. "No one knows."

Morag **sighs**. This trip to the bakery is taking a very long time.

"The strange thing is," continues Mrs Ross, "They haven't even found his dog, a little black and white one called Dougal."

Morag's heart bangs loudly. Her **attention** is suddenly completely focused on what the two old ladies are saying. Morag runs out of the bakery, all thoughts of fresh bread forgotten. She needs to tell Dad! With shaking hands Morag **grabs** her bike, jumps on and cycles off as fast as she can. Her teeth bang together as her bicyle **bumps** onto the road. The wind blows her ginger hair into her eyes. Quickly she brushes it out of her face with one hand as she cycles round a parked car.

"WOAH!"

attention	Aufmerksamkeit
to grab sth.	greifen, (sich) schnappen
to bump	stoßen, aufschlagen

Exercise 2: Translation. Übersetzen Sie die Wörter ins Englische!

1. This trip to the Bäckerei ________________ is taking a very long time.
2. Every Saturday she cycled to the next Dorf ________________ to buy fresh bread Brötchen ________________.
3. A Wanderer ________________ is missing in the hills.
4. The lady at the front of the Schlange ________________ can't sich entscheiden ________________ what to buy.
5. Morag sich schnappen ________________ her bike to get home as fast as she can.

Morag **slams on her brakes** and stops just in time. She nearly runs into a young mother with her baby.

to slam on the brakes	eine Vollbremsung machen
angrily	wütend, verärgert
familiar	bekannt, vertraut
to gasp	keuchen, schnaufen
breathless	atemlos
emergency	Notfall

"Sorry!" shouts Morag

"Watch where you're going!" the lady says **angrily**.

Morag is shocked and forgets for a moment why she is in such a hurry. But then she remembers. Dougal! The missing hiker! She must tell Dad! Morag puts her head down and pedals quickly. As she comes around the side of the primary school Morag sees a **familiar** figure in a black uniform. It is the village policeman.

"Sergeant[i] Campbell! Sergeant Campbell!" cries Morag.

The policeman turns around as Morag stops her bicycle right in front of him.

"Sergeant Campbell!" **gasps** Morag.

"Yes," the policeman looks down at the hot and **breathless** young girl on her bicycle. "How can I help you?"

"The dog!" cries Morag. "We found the dog!"

"What?" asks Sergeant Campbell. "You've found a dog?" He laughs. "I thought you were going to tell me about an **emergency**."

Sergeant bzw. *Police Constable* ist der höchste von 4 Polizeirängen in Großbritannien. Darunter folgen *Inspector, Superintendent* sowie *Assistant Chief Constable*. Achtung, es wird ganz anders ausgesprochen als es geschrieben wird, und zwar: **ˈsɑːdʒənt**

"No! Not a dog. We found THE dog!"

"The dog?"

The policeman sighs and looks closely at Morag.

"You're Farmer McKay's daughter aren't you?"

"Yes, Morag," she gasps, still breathless.
"Okay young lady," says Sergeant Campbell. "Calm down and tell me what the problem is."
Morag takes a deep breath.
"We've found the missing hiker's dog."
Sergeant Campbell's eyebrows go up in surprise.
"You're sure?"
"Absolutely," she says.

Exercise 3: True or false. Welche Aussagen sind korrekt? Markieren Sie mit richtig ✓ oder falsch — und korrigieren Sie die falschen Aussagen!

1. The McKay's live in the middle of a village. ❐
2. Morag has long, blonde hair. ❐
3. The policeman is wearing a blue uniform. ❐
4. Morag knows one of the old ladies in the queue from church. ❐
5. It is winter when the hiker goes missing. ❐

"He suddenly **appeared** in our **farmyard** last night. We thought he was lost so we kept him in our kitchen all night. We wanted to try and find his owner today."

to appear	erscheinen, auftauchen
farmyard	Bauernhof
to belong to sb.	jmd. gehören

"Why do you think the dog **belongs to** the missing hiker?" asks the policeman.

"Well, he's small, black and white and the name on his collar is Dougal."
"Dougal!"
"Yes," says Morag, "... and I heard some ladies in the bakery just now saying that there is a missing walker and that his dog is called Dougal."
Sergeant Campbell looks **excited**.
"It sounds like he really could be our missing dog." He smiles at her. "Well done Morag!"
Morag smiles back.
"Right, here is what we're going to do," **explains** the policeman. "You go home and tell your father what has happened. I will ring **headquarters** and contact the Mountain Rescue Team."
Morag **nods**.

excited	aufgeregt, begeistert
to explain	erklären
head-quarters *pl*	*hier:* die Zentrale
to nod	nicken
lane	*hier:* kleine ländliche Straße
gate	Tor
muddy	schlammig
to jump	*hier:* zusammenzucken

"Okay, now go home," says Sergeant Campbell. "But be careful. We don't need any more accidents!"
Morag puts her foot on her pedal as Sergeant Campbell turns to hurry back to the police station. At the last minute he calls over his shoulder.
"Oh and Morag, don't let that dog escape! He's our best chance of finding the missing walker."

Morag pedals back to the farm as fast as she can. The trees along the **lane** seem to fly by.
She turns through the open **gate** into the **muddy** farmyard. Her bike slips on the ground as she brakes hard. She throws

her bike to the ground by the farmhouse door and runs into the kitchen.

"Dad! Dad!" she shouts.

"Woah, where's the fire!" exclaims Mr McKay with a laugh.

He is standing at the kitchen sink washing his hands. Dougal is on the floor by his feet. Every now and again he whimpers unhappily.

"Dad, I know who Dougal's owner is!" cries Morag.

Mr McKay looks at his daughter in surprise. Her cheeks are pink and she looks excited.

"That's excellent news," he replies. "How did you find out?"

Morag throws herself on to one of the wooden chairs at the kitchen table. She feels tired from her cycle ride. Dougal walks over to her. She strokes the top of his head.

"Well, I was in the bakery and I heard two ladies talking about a missing hiker..."

Mr McKay listens as his daughter explains everything that happened while she was in the village. At that moment the telephone rings. The noise makes them both **jump**. In two big steps he crosses the kitchen and picks up the phone.

Exercise 4: Opposites. **Wie lautet das Gegenteil? Ordnen Sie zu!**

1. ☐ lost	a) closed
2. ☐ open	b) terrible
3. ☐ excited	c) found
4. ☐ excellent	d) main road
5. ☐ lane	e) bored

"Hello?" he shouts into the phone. "Yes, this is Mr McKay."

He turns suddenly to look at Morag. "Oh, hello Sergeant Campbell. Yes, my daughter told me she spoke to you."

to rescue	retten
to work out	*hier:* etw. herausfinden
to pace	auf- und abgehen
unlikely	unwahrscheinlich
to survive	überleben
serious	ernst(haft)
bravely	tapfer, mutig
permission	Erlaubnis
to arrive	ankommen

Morag sinks back into her chair and relaxes. The policeman will fix everything. Everything will be okay. The man will be **rescued** soon.

"What?" exclaims Mr McKay in shock.

The voice on the other end of the phone is speaking quickly and without pausing. Morag is listening carefully, trying to **work out** what Sergeant Campbell is saying. Her dad is **pacing** the floor, holding the phone to his ear. He is clearly worried.

"It's **unlikely**!" says Mr McKay into the phone. "That poor man has been out there all night. He must be very cold. I'm not sure how much longer he can **survive**."

The voice on the phone begins to speak quickly again.

"One minute," says Mr McKay to Sergeant Campbell.

Mr McKay gives his daughter a very **serious** look.

"Morag, shall we go and search for him together?"

Morag nods **bravely**.

"Right," says Mr McKay into the phone. "My daughter and I will go out now to look for him. We know these hills and may be able to find him before you get here."

Sergeant Campbell's voice gets louder.

"I'm not asking for your **permission**," says Mr McKay.

"I'm telling you what we're doing. I've got my mobile phone so we can keep in contact. Ring me as soon as you **arrive**."

Morag's dad quickly ends the call and hangs up the phone.
"Morag, it looks like you were right. Dougal and his owner Mr McGregor have been missing since yesterday. People have been out overnight looking for him. He told his wife that he was going walking near Loch Karon[i]."
"That's about twenty miles away!" says Morag **confused**.
"That's right," says her dad. "Perhaps he **changed his mind** about where he was going for a walk. It is very unlikely that Dougal could find his way here from so far away. His owner must be somewhere in the hills behind the farm."

confused	verwirrt
to change one's mind	es sich anders überlegen
whole	ganz, gesamt
several	einige

"They've been looking for him in the wrong place then!" exclaims Morag.
"It looks like it. Sergeant Campbell said that the Mountain Rescue Team spent the **whole** night in the hills around Loch Karon. He's contacted them and they're going to come to us now. But they'll need **several** hours to walk down from the hills and then to drive here."

Loch ist der schottische Begriff für einen See. Das wohl berühmteste Beispiel ist Loch Ness, im Norden Schottlands, in dem angeblich das Seeungeheuer Nessie wohnt.

Now Morag understands why her father is worried.
"The policeman wanted us to stay here and wait for them."
"We can't do that," says Morag standing up.
"That's what I said. Now quick, we need to get ready as fast as we can."
"What do we need?" asks Morag, trying to sound less nervous than she feels.

Exercise 5: Contracted forms. Wie lautet die verkürzte Form?

1. we will *we'll*

2. that is ____________

3. they are ____________

4. cannot ____________

5. they have ____________

Twenty minutes later Morag and her father are closing the door of the farmhouse behind them. They are dressed warmly in waterproof jackets, thick sweaters and walking boots. In the rucksacks on their backs they have hot tea, food, blankets and a **first aid kit**. Mr McKay is holding a piece of **rope** that is now tied to Dougal's collar. The little dog is pulling on the rope. He can't wait to get going.

first aid kit	Erstehilfekasten
rope	Seil
path	Weg, Pfad
steep	steil

"Slow down Dougal," says Mr McKay. "We could have a long way to go."

The **path** from the farmhouse and up into the hills is **steep** and rocky. Soon they can look down on the farmhouse. Morag can see their sheep in the fields.
"Look how small they seem," she says to her dad.
The sun is now shining from a blue sky with just a few little

white clouds. The hills are covered with purple **heather** as far as they can see. But **in the distance,** the hills are so high they still have white snow on the tops.

They have been walking for about an hour when Mr McKay says, "Look Morag!"

Morag looks to where her father is pointing. On the hillside above them there is a **herd of deer.** The beautiful, big animals are watching them. Morag can see several male deer with huge **antlers** on their heads.

heather	Erika (Heidekraut)
in the distance	in der Ferne
herd of deer *pl*	Hirschrudel
antlers *pl*	Geweih
to scare	erschrecken
to be lucky	Glück haben
to bark	bellen

"Sssh Dougal," whispers her dad.

He doesn't want Dougal to **scare** the deer so he is holding the rope very tightly.

Suddenly the herd of deer start to run. Morag and her father watch until they have all gone over the hill and they can no longer see them.

"Wow," says Morag.

"Yes," replies her father. "We were **lucky** to see them."

Dougal **barks**.

"You're right Dougal," says her dad. "We've got a job to do. Let's find your owner."

The small dog looks up at them.

"I think he understands," says Morag.

Dougal suddenly turns off the path.

"Are you sure that's the way?" asks Morag. "The path is easier."

Dougal barks.

"I think that's a yes," laughs Mr McKay.

The small dog pulls on his rope.

"Let's go," says Morag.

It is difficult to walk in the heather. They have to be very careful where they put their feet so they don't fall.
"Can you see anyone?" Mr McKay asks his daughter.
"No," replies Morag. "But look at Dougal. He is very excited."
Dougal seems to know exactly where he is going.
"Mr McGregor!" shouts dad. "Can you hear us?"
They listen. All they can hear is the wind and some birds in the distance.

eventually	endlich, schließlich
bite	Biss(en)
to promise	versprechen
impatiently	ungeduldig
to sniff	*hier:* schnüffeln
hare	Hase

"Mr McGregor!" calls Morag.
Nothing.
"I think we should stop for a rest," says dad **eventually**.
They sit down together on a rock. Mr McKay takes some sandwiches out of his rucksack and hands them to Morag.
"How are you feeling my love?"
Morag takes a big **bite** of her sandwich.
"I'm okay. My legs are a little tired but I can keep walking."
She can see that her dad is worried about the missing hiker. She doesn't want him to worry about her too.
"I'm okay, I **promise**."
"Good girl."
Dougal is waiting **impatiently**. They start to pack their bags again, but then Mr McKay's mobile phone rings.
"Hello?"
It's Sergeant Campbell. Morag listens as her dad explains where they are.
"We haven't found Mr McGregor yet, but we're still looking. Dougal seems to know where he is going."
He ends the call and turns to Morag.

Exercise 6: Questions about the text. Beantworten Sie die Fragen zum Text!

1. What animals do Morag, her Dad and Dougal see?

____

2. What colour is heather?

____

3. What do Morag and her father eat on their walk?

____

4. What is the path from the farmhouse up into the hills like?

____

5. What can Morag and her father hear?

____

"Mountain Rescue are down from the mountains near Loch Karon now. They will be at our farm soon," he explains.
Morag stands up.
"Let's see if we can find Dougal's owner before they arrive," she says. "Then we can tell them where to go."
Morag and her father follow Dougal across the heather. The little dog keeps his nose to the ground, **sniffing** as he walks. Suddenly a mountain **hare** jumps out of the heather just in front of them.

"Eek!" cries Morag in shock.
The hare jumps across the heather. It moves very fast on its **powerful** legs. Dougal seems to forget what he is doing for a moment and tries to run after the hare.

powerful	kräftig
valley	Tal
stream	Fluss, Bach

"Woah Dougal," says dad, pulling on the rope.
A horrible thought comes into Morag's head.

Exercise 7: Spot the mistakes. Lesen Sie weiter und identifizieren Sie die acht Fehler im folgenden Abschnitt!

"Think you he is taking us to his owner Dad?" she asks. "Perhaps he just following the smell of animals."
"I don't hope so," says Morags dad. "I'am not sure how we will finding Mr McGregor without Dougal."
Morag bends down to talk at the small dog.
"Can you help us Dougal? Can you show us the way?"
Dougal bark in reply.

"Let's keep going," says Mr McKay.
They follow Dougal round the side of the hill. The dog is walking faster and faster and starts barking excitedly. Morag has to hurry to keep up.
"I wonder if we're close," asks Morag.
"Mr McGregor!" shouts her dad. "Mr McGregor!"
There is no reply.
"Mr McGregor!" calls Morag. "Can you hear us?"
They walk – almost running – down the side of a small **valley** with a **stream** at the bottom.

to untie	losbinden
to disappear	verschwinden
to yell	brüllen
moan	Stöhnen

They call again. "Mr McGregor! Mr McGregor!"
Dougal is now barking loudly and pulling hard on his rope.
"Mr McGregor!" shouts Mr McKay.
"Maybe we should let Dougal go free?" says Morag.
"Good idea."
Dad **unties** the rope from Dougal's collar and the small dog runs quickly towards the stream.
"Follow him!" cries Morag.
They hurry down the hill after Dougal. He is walking round in circles and sniffing the ground by the side of the stream. He runs through the stream and up the other side of the little valley. His black and white body suddenly **disappears** behind some rocks.
"DOUGAL!" shouts Morag.
"Mr McGregor!" **yells** her dad.
They can hear lots of loud barking and then a low **moan**.
"Did you hear that?" asks dad excitedly.
The moan came again.
"Have we found the missing hiker?"
"Let's go and see," says Mr McKay.
They hurry across the stream and up to the rocks, then round the rocks and there he is!
"Mr McGregor!" cries Morag.
The missing hiker is lying on his side. His eyes are closed and he is not moving. Morag feels panicked. What should they do now?
Mr McKay kneels down beside the man. He touches his face.
"Mr McGregor, can you hear me? We're here to help you."

Mr McGregor makes another moan.
Dad quickly looks all over the man to see if he is hurt.
"I think his leg may be broken, Morag."
The hiker's foot is at an unnatural **angle**. Morag feels a bit strange when she looks at it.
"That must be why he couldn't get home," says Morag.
"Yes, it looks like it. He's very lucky Dougal came to find help. Without that little dog it is very unlikely we would be here!"
Mr McGregor moans again.
"Morag," says Mr McKay turning to his daughter. "Hurry, get the blanket out of my rucksack. He is very cold. We need to warm him up."
Morag puts the blanket over the hiker and **tucks** it under his body. She is very careful not to move his **injured** leg. Dougal lies next to his owner. Morag gently strokes the dog's head.

angle	Winkel
to tuck	stecken, einklemmen
injured	verletzt
barely conscious	kaum bei Bewusstsein
finally	endlich
relieved	erleichtert

"He's **barely conscious**," says Mr McKay. "We need to get some help here quickly. You stay with him. I'm going to walk up to the top of the hill to ring Sergeant Campbell. I will get a better signal there."
"Okay Dad." Morag nods but feels a bit scared about staying by herself with the man. She watches as her dad walks away.
Two hours later Morag is sitting alone at the top of the hill. Mr McKay sent her to look out for the rescuers. She looks at her watch. The Mountain Rescue Team should be here at any moment. She hopes so. She is starting to feel very cold and tired. Suddenly there they are!

Exercise 8: Hidden words. In diesem Gitternetz sind zehn Wörter versteckt, die mit der Rettungsaktion von Morag und ihrem Vater zu tun haben. Finden Sie sie!

W	A	T	E	R	P	R	O	O	F
R	N	T	A	O	I	O	N	L	I
U	G	B	H	P	E	P	U	N	R
C	R	E	S	C	U	E	I	F	S
K	R	A	E	Z	U	N	E	R	T
S	W	E	A	T	E	R	O	A	A
A	J	G	R	V	P	E	S	N	I
C	J	A	C	K	E	T	M	K	D
K	U	T	H	S	T	R	E	A	K
O	I	N	J	U	R	E	D	G	I
Y	O	R	B	L	A	N	K	E	T

"Hello! Over here!" shouts Morag.
She stands up and waves her dad's red waterproof jacket to get their attention. The team is still a long way away. Can they see her?
"Hello!" she shouts again, waving and jumping up and down.
Finally one of the team sees her and waves back. Morag is so **relieved**! The team of six walk to meet Morag.
"We're so happy we found you," says the blonde lady at the

front. "My name is Alice. I'm the team leader. You must be Morag. Can you show us where the injured man is please?"
"He's down here," replies Morag.
The team follow her down the hill to the rocks by the little stream. Dougal barks and Mr McKay stands up to greet them.
"Hello, I'm very glad to see you!" he says.
"So are we!" laughs one of the men in a red hat. "It has been a very long night!"
Alice and her team quickly move to look at the injured man. While the others get out the **equipment** they will need, one of the Mountain Rescue Team speaks to Mr McGregor.

equipment	Ausrüstung
medic	Sanitäter
hypothermia	Unterkühlung
air ambulance	Luftrettungs-dienst
to secure	*hier:* fixieren
stretcher	Tragbahre
calmly	ruhig, gelassen

"Hello Sir, my name is Angus," he says loudly. "I am a **medic**. I'm just going to have a good look at you. Then we will get you out of here."
Angus pulls back the blanket and starts to examine him. He asks Mr McGregor lots of questions but the injured man can't answer. Mr McGregor moans when Angus touches his leg.
"Sorry Sir," says Angus. "I'm finished now. Try to relax."
He puts the blanket back around Mr McGregor and comes over to speak quietly to Alice. She is standing with Morag and Mr McKay.
"He definitely has a bad leg injury," says Angus. "He also has **hypothermia** from being out all night. We need to get him to the hospital as quickly as possible."
"Right," says Alice. "I'll call for the **air ambulance**. They can fly him to hospital quicker than we can carry him off the hills."

Quickly she begins to speak into her radio while Angus **secures** Mr McGregor's injured leg. The rest of the team make a **stretcher** out of bits of bright orange plastic.
"An air ambulance?" Morag asks her father.
"A helicopter," he explains.
The Mountain Rescue Team gently move Mr McGregor on to the stretcher.
"We need to carry him up to the top of the hill," explains Alice, "so the helicopter has space to land."
Morag and her Dad follow the team as they carry the injured man across the stream and up the side of the valley. Dougal walks **calmly** by their side. He seems to understand that everyone is here to help his owner.
"You're such a clever dog!" says Morag.

Exercise 9: Verb forms. Wie lauten das Present Simple und Past Simple der folgenden Verben in der dritten Person?

1. follow *follows* ____ *followed* ____
2. carry ____ ____
3. greet ____ ____
4. touch ____ ____
5. try ____ ____

Finally in the distance they can hear the sound of the helicopter getting louder and louder as it flies closer.

"Where is it?" asks Mr McKay impatiently.
"There it is," cries Morag. "I can see it!"
They all watch as the bright yellow helicopter appears over the hill.
"Keep down," says Alice.
Morag and her dad stay sitting in the heather as they watch the helicopter land on the hilltop. They can see the pilot in the cockpit. He gives them a quick wave. Morag can't believe how **noisy** the helicopter is! Or how the wind from the **rotor blades flattens** the heather all around it.
They watch as the Mountain Rescue Team carry Mr McGregor up the hill on the stretcher. They quickly put the stretcher into the helicopter, shut its doors and hurry back down the hill. The rotor blades begin to rotate. The Mountain Rescue Team, Morag and her father all stand and watch as the helicopter takes off and flies away. The whole rescue has only taken a few minutes.
"Wow!" says Mr McKay. "That is something you don't see every day!"

noisy	laut
rotor blades *pl*	Rotorblätter
to flatten	*hier:* flach drücken

The long walk back to the farmhouse feels like it will never end. Morag is very tired and cold. They follow Alice, Angus and the rest of the Mountain Rescue Team down the hills. Morag holds her father's big, warm hand as they walk down the rocky path. She thinks if she lets

> Die einfache Form der Zukunft **will + Infinitiv** (future simple oder will future) wird benutzt für:
> a) Ereignisse und vage Abischten, die noch weit in der Zukunft liegen
> b) Vermutungen und Dinge, die ohne Ihren Einfluss passieren werden

go she might fall. Mr McKay has Dougal's rope in his other hand.
"Keep going, my girl," he whispers. "We're nearly home."

amazed	erstaunt
vehicle	Fahrzeug
crowd	(Menschen-)Menge
chicken coop	Hühnerstall
bucket	Eimer
to feed	füttern

Morag can only nod. She is so tired.
Finally they can see the farmhouse! It looks so small at first, but as they get closer Morag can see lots of cars in the farmyard. What is going on? Morag, Mr McKay and the Mountain Rescue Team finally walk through the big farm gate into the yard. Morag is **amazed**. The farmyard is full of cars and people.
"Who are all these people Dad?"
She can see the Mountain Rescue vans, two police cars and other **vehicles** she doesn't know. In the **crowd** she sees Sergeant Campbell. He is talking to a small man with a camera and a notebook.
"Hello!" cries Sergeant Campbell. "Well done everyone. I have heard that Mr McGregor has arrived at hospital. His leg is broken but he is going to be okay."
"Everyone, I am from the Daily News," says the small man. "Can you all stand together so I can take a photograph please."

It is a few days later and Morag is walking up the hill from the **chicken coop**. The metal food **bucket** is banging against her leg. **Feeding** the chickens is her favourite after-school job. She loves the mad, noisy birds.
When Morag walks around the corner of the farmhouse she finds a familiar[i] face waiting for her in the yard.

Achtung!
familiar ≠ familiär
familiar = vertraut, bekannt
informal, personal = familiär

Exercise 10: Object pronouns. Ersetzen Sie die fett gedruckten Wörter durch Pronomen!

1. They follow **Alice, Angus and the rest of the Mountain Rescue Team** down the hills.

   They follow them down the hills.

2. If she lets go of **his hand** she might fall.

   ____

3. Mr McKay tells **Morag** to keep going.

   ____

4. She sees **Sergeant Campbell** in the crowd.

   ____

5. He wants to take a photograph of **me, you and the team.**

   ____

"Dougal!" she cries in surprise.

The little dog's tail is **wagging** as he runs over to her. Morag kneels down and puts her arms around him.

"What are you doing here?" she asks aloud.

Dougal **gives her** cheek a big wet **lick**!

"Urgh, Dougal!" laughs Morag.

The farmhouse door opens. Mr McKay is standing in the doorway. His big body fills the space.

"Come inside you two," he says smiling.

Morag is confused, but she follows her father into the house with Dougal. There is a lady standing in the kitchen with a big cup of tea in her hand. Morag doesn't know her.

"Hello my dear," says the lady with a big grin on her face. "My name is Mrs McGregor."

to wag	wedeln
to give sb. a lick	jmd. ablecken
grateful	dankbar
shyly	schüchtern
headline	Schlagzeile
proud	stolz
adventure	Abenteuer

Morag looks at her father. His kind eyes are smiling.

"I want to say thank you to you and your father," says Mrs McGregor with tears in her eyes. "I can't tell you how **grateful** I am for everything you did. You saved my husband's life."

Morag doesn't know what to say. She smiles **shyly** at her visitor. Mr McKay puts his hand gently on Mrs McGregor's shoulder and leads her to a seat at the kitchen table.

"Come and sit down Morag."

They all sit at the table. Dougal lies down under Morag's chair. The local newspaper from the day after the rescue is still on the table. There is a photograph of Morag, her dad and Dougal with the Mountain Rescue Team.

The **headline** reads 'Highland Heroes!' It still makes Morag smile. She feels very **proud**.

"Now," says Mrs McGregor, "I want to know everything. Tell me all about your **adventure**."

Her dad smiles at Morag.

"Go on love, you were the one who found Dougal and worked out how to find Mr McGregor."

"Well," says Morag, "Where do I start...?"

Time for a Change

Sarah Trenker

Zwei Welten treffen aufeinander: Edward Dixon arbeitet in Brighton als Sachbearbeiter im Jobcenter und führt ein strikt geregeltes Leben. Eines Tages wird er mit einem scheinbar hoffnungslosen Fall konfrontiert: Die chaotische Denise Shepherd hält es nie länger als ein paar Wochen im selben Job aus. Edward sieht es als Herausforderung, die junge Frau wieder auf den rechten Weg zu bringen. Doch wird er diesen ultimativen Test bestehen?

Edward Dixon liebt Ordnung und Routine. Er trägt gebügelte Hemden, hat eine geregelte Arbeit und ein geordnetes Leben. Bei seinen Kollegen ist er eher als Schlaftablette bekannt – mit der Ausnahme von Sandra, mit der er eng zusammenarbeitet und die ihn gerne für seinen Ordnungswahn aufzieht.

Denise Shepherd ist jung, schön und hat einen Oxford Abschluss in der Tasche. Ihre Mutter ist eine bekannte und wohlhabende TV-Persönlichkeit. Obwohl ihr damit die Welt zu Füßen liegen könnte, hat sie sich ihr ganz eigenes Lebensziel gesetzt.

Sandra Roberts, Edwards junge rothaarige Kollegin, ist gerade zum zweiten Mal Mutter geworden. Sie ist spontan, lebendig und ein richtiger Spaßvogel.

"Edward, I have a question for you."
Edward is busy organizing his pens and pencils in a line on his desk. He always does that after he starts the computer. Then he puts the telephone back where it should be. The cleaning lady never leaves it in the same place. Edward likes things to be **shipshape** on his desk. It is part of his daily routine, and – as he often tells people – you should never change a good routine. He turns his head to Sandra, who is sitting at the desk next to his in the big **open-plan office**.

ϟ **shipshape**	tipptopp
open-plan office	Großraumbüro
to snort	schnauben, prusten
however	jedoch, allerdings
mug	Becher
probably	wahrscheinlich

"Yes? What is it?"
Sandra points down at her desk: "Are you happy with your life?"
Edward **snorts**. His young colleague is always reading women's magazines on the way to work. Her desk is full of them, too, as well as papers, pencils – NOT in a line! – and yellow Post-it notes. Edward can't understand how Brenda can work in such chaos. At the moment, **however**, she is not working. She is looking at him and drinking tea from an Ed Sheeran **mug**.
The question is clearly from one of her magazines, Edward thinks. **Probably** another article telling you that you are happy or sad, too fat or too thin, drink too much or too little and whether you do enough sport.
"Sandra, it is 8 a.m. on Monday morning at the Brighton job centre. There are a lot of people in front of the building who don't have jobs. In half an hour they will all come in to see us. Why don't you ask them if they are happy?"
Sandra grins. "Because I'm asking you."

"Okay, well I'm happy that I have a job," Says Edward, going back to his pens and pencils, which are still not 100% yet. Then he looks at Sandra again. She is staring at him with that look on her face that says: "What a **strange** man you are". Edward **sighs** and stands up to go and get his coffee. What is wrong with lining up your pencils? Or covering all your books with brown paper? He lines up the **tins** of Campbell's soups in his kitchen cupboard at home, too. In the bathroom his toothbrush glass and soap are always at a right angle to the **sink**.

strange	merkwürdig, seltsam
to sigh	seufzen
tin	*hier:* Dose
sink	Spülbecken
waste of time	Zeitverschwendung
to play a trick on sb.	jmd. einen Streich spielen
to shake sb. out of sth.	*hier:* jmd. wachrütteln
weird	seltsam, sonderbar
actually	eigentlich
queue	(Warte-)Schlange
especially	besonders
diary	*hier:* Terminkalender

Order and routine help him through the day. And that is a reason to be happy. Not that he ever asks himself if he is *really* happy or if life is *really* good. Why should he? What a **waste of time**. Life is life. When nothing too bad happens, it is good. And when something bad happens, you just deal with it, don't you? It is never nice when his dog does 'something' in front of a restaurant when people are eating. And he wasn't happy when his wife left him for one of his few friends. But that's life. Worse things can happen, as he well knows. It is far better to live with a dog that loves you than a wife who doesn't. When he comes back to his desk with his coffee, Sandra tries a simpler question. "Did you have a nice weekend?"
"Yes, very nice, thank you," he replies with a smile. Sandra

smiles, too. Edward likes Sandra. The young, red-haired woman, who has just come back to work after her second child, is a real bundle of energy. She laughs a lot – sometimes a bit too much for Edward – and is always **playing tricks** on him. When he goes to get his coffee, she sometimes moves his pencils or his notebook. He knows that it is because Sandra wants to **shake** him **out of** his old-man routine. He once heard her talking about him in the kitchen: "Yes, he is a bit **weird**, but he is **actually** a really nice person. I like him a lot. And he is good at his job. He finds many jobs for people who really want one. It doesn't matter how old they are or what qualifications they have."

Exercise 1: Prepositions. Setzen Sie die richtige Präpositionen ein!

in by on on ~~at~~ at

The job centre always opens **1.** _at_ 8.30 a.m. **2.** ________ the time the manager of the job centre, Kevin Rochester, arrives **3.** ________ work, the **queue** on the road is very long. There are people sitting **4.** ________ the waiting areas and **5.** ________ the steps outside the centre. It is **especially** busy **6.** ________ Mondays.

Edward looks at his **diary**. Mondays at the job centre are always difficult. A lot of problem people come here on Mondays. There are people who don't really want a job but **pretend** that they are looking for one. George Butler and Jayne Johnston are two good examples. They often say they don't want to do the job he has for them. They say that it is not good enough. Edward finds it hard to keep smiling on such days. The only positive thing about this Monday so far is that Jayne Johnston hasn't come in today. She still has the job at the supermarket. However, there is a message from the supermarket manager on Edward's desk, so he is not too optimistic. But George Butler is back sitting in front of him with a long face.

to pretend	etw. vorgeben, vortäuschen
waiter	Bedienung
to expect	erwarten
surprised	überrascht
to continue to do sth.	weitermachen, fortfahren

"So Mr Butler, why are you already back here? What is wrong with working at the restaurant? You like people, don't you?"
"Yes, but they all want something from me."
"You're a **waiter** (i). What do you **expect**?"
"And then I have to start so early."
"Early?! You start at 10 a.m."
George Butler looks **surprised**. "But I don't usually get up until 9 a.m. I need my sleep"
Edward looks at his watch. "But you are working today, I hope...?"
Mr Butler looks down at his feet. Edward can't believe it. "When I make little mistakes, Mr Forte gets so angry. I don't think he wants me to come to work today."
"And tomorrow?"
George Butler **continues** to look at his feet.

Mit der Endung **-er** kann man aus vielen Verben Substantive bilden. Zum Beispiel:
waiter viewer, writer, player

"What are *little* mistakes, Mr Butler?"

"Well, for example, when the soup **plates** are very hot, it is difficult to hold them, and – well – there was a lady at the table who..."

plate	Teller
Great Dane	Dogge

"Okay. I don't want to hear the details," Edward says, sighing. He clicks on his computer and starts to look for[i] another job for Mr Butler.

Exercise 2: Verb forms. Wie lautet das Present Simple und Past Simple der folgenden Verben in der dritten Person?

1. to be *is* *was*

2. to say ________ ________

3. to reply ________ ________

4. to continue ________ ________

5. to shake ________ ________

6. to make ________ ________

At midday, Edward takes his jacket and his bike and cycles to Mrs Mitchell's house. Mrs Mitchell, his next-door neighbour, looks after his **Great Dane** Minnie during the day. But at 91 she can no longer go out. So Edward al-

> Im Englischen gibt es mehr als 3000 Phrasal Verbs, bestehend aus Verb + Partikel (Adverb oder Präposition). Der Partikel kann die Bedeutung des Verbs vollkommen ändern, z.B.:
> **to look for** (suchen)
> **to look after** (sich kümmern)
> **to look forward to** (sich freuen auf)

ways rides home at lunchtime to take Minnie for a quick walk round the park.
"You look like I feel," Mrs Mitchell says when she sees Edward. "I won't ask you if your morning was fun."
"I hate Mondays," Edward says as he calls Minnie. "As I often say, it is difficult to **meet** everyone's **expectations**."
"**Perhaps** some people just expect too much," Mrs Mitchell replies – as she always does.

to meet (sb.'s) expectations	Erwartungen erfüllen
perhaps	vielleicht

"Have a good walk. Would you like me to make you a cheese and Marmite sandwich?"
"That would be perfect, Mrs Mitchell, thank you," answers Edward – as he always does.
Minnie likes walking Edward around the park. Sometimes she finds him a bit slow, especially when she wants to say hello to other dogs. But she loves her two-legged friend and usually runs to him when he calls. Okay, sometimes she takes a little longer if something smells very nice, or if there is another dog she wants to say hello to. But she never lets him shout for too long.

When Edward gets back to the office, Sandra picks up her big pink bag to go out for her lunch.
"The boss wants you to go to his office," she says. "I think he has somebody 'nice' for you."
"Oh, how *nice* of him." Edward puts the plate with his cheese and Marmite sandwich on his desk. He looks at Sandra and has to smile. "Is there any chance that you would like to have the 'somebody nice'...?"
Sandra laughs loudly as she walks through the door.

Exercise 3: Odd one out. **Unterstreichen Sie das Wort, das nicht in die Reihe passt!**

1. kitchen bathroom bedroom office
2. plate glass mug cup
3. pencil pen desk rubber
4. neighbour boss manager chief
5. smells meets sounds feels
6. optimistic hopeful positive angry

"You know he loves me even more than he loves you. While you were out, he gave me a wonderful project, too." Still laughing, Sandra closes the door.

Edward puts his computer back on. Sandra is right. Kevin Rochester, the manager of the job centre, does not like Edward, but he really hates Sandra. Edward knows why. It is because Sandra is a **threat**. She is young and very good at her job, and everybody on the team likes her. This is not true of Kevin Rochester.

threat	Bedrohung, Gefahr
broad	breit
moustache	Schnurrbart

Kevin Rochester is an ex-army officer who still thinks that he is in the army. He is a tall man, with **broad** shoulders and a **moustache**. He was a very good officer because he loved his work. He does not like his work at the job centre, so he is a very bad manager. He is only good at shouting and making sure that everyone knows that he is the boss.

When Edward goes into his office, he knows what to expect from Kevin Rochester.

"So, Dixon, where were you all this time?"

Edward hates the way Mr Rochester calls all the men by their surnames (i) and all the women by their first names.

nasty	gemein, fies
degree	Studienabschluss
advisor	Berater/in
to get on well with sb.	sich mit jdm. gut verstehen
to explain	erklären
to slam	*hier:* knallen
to disagree	widersprechen, anderer Meinung sein

"Mrs Roberts tells me that you have something for me."

Kevin Rochester has a **nasty** smile on his face. "Yes, I do."

He holds up a piece of paper and Edward takes it.

"Denise Shepherd. 25. **Degree** in English Literature from Oxford University. She is a writer, so it should be easy to find a job for her. But Miss Shepherd seems to get bored quickly. Four jobs, four **advisors**. The last one was Ted Banner. He doesn't want to deal with her again. He says she is weird – which is why I think you will both **get on very well**... Her mother is that TV woman Rosemary Shepherd, which probably **explains** why she is weird."

(i) Im englischsprachigen Raum spricht man sich üblicherweise viel schneller mit dem Vornamen an als in Deutschland, aber Achtung: die Verwendung des Vornamens bedeutet nicht automatisch persönliche Nähe und definitiv nicht gleich Freundschaft.

"She actually helps a lot of people," Edward says quietly. "I don't know what's 'weird' about that."

Edward's boss **slams** the papers on the desk. Kevin Rochester doesn't like it when people **disagree** with him. "Remember to read the **back**

page. It's a summary of all the jobs the young lady is too good for. She is coming in at 2 p.m. This is the job Banner selected for her. See what she says. I want to hear how it goes. That's all."

back page	Rückseite (des Blatts)
job seeker	Arbeits-suchender
proud	stolz
to fit into	hineinpassen
usually	normalerweise

Edward has to stop himself from shouting, "Yes, sir!" He thinks that Kevin Rochester probably doesn't understand sarcasm.

Exercise 4: Opposites. Wie lautet das Gegenteil der folgenden Adjektive?

1. nasty *nice* ____________

2. normal ____________

3. interested ____________

4. loud ____________

5. thin ____________

Back in his office, Edward takes off his jacket and sits down at his desk. He reads the information about Denise Shepherd. He is surprised. She does not fall into any of his four categories of **job seeker**. Edward is quite **proud** of his categories, because every job seeker **fits into** one of them... **usually**. The categories cover a lot of different things. His "Too Young/Old" category, for example, is not just about how old people are. It is about qualifications and how good they are at interviews. But Denise Shepherd has a whole list of jobs, so interviews are clearly not a problem, and her qualifications are very good. At 25, with a degree from Oxford University, she is a perfect age and top candidate. The number of jobs shows that **laziness** (i) is also not a problem.

laziness	Faulheit
challenge	Herausforderung
to drop sth.	etw. fallen lassen
relative	Verwandte/r
unfortunate	unglücklich
to raise one's eyebrows	die Stirn runzeln

"Yes, she is a **challenge**," Edward thinks.

The telephone rings. It is Alfredo Forte from the Italian restaurant. He is not at all happy with Edward. He has lost one of his best customers because George Butler **dropped** a bowl of minestrone soup on Mrs Mason. He makes it clear that if Edward sends someone like that again, he will send some of his **relatives** from Palermo to drop something on him.

At 2 p.m., when Denise walks through the door, she can see that her new advisor at the job centre is not having a good day. The tall, thin man in his early thirties is standing behind his desk. He is holding a telephone and talking to somebody at the other end of the line.

Bei Wörtern die auf „**y**" enden, wird bei einer Wortbildung mit neuem Suffix das „y" zu einem „i":

lazy	laz**iness**
pretty	prett**ier**
happy	happ**iness**

"Yes, Mr Forte. I do understand. It was very **unfortunate**."

Mr Dixon waits for a second, holding the phone away from his ear. He looks at Denise and **raises his** thick black **eyebrows**. He points at the chair opposite his desk and says quietly, "Please sit down".

"Mr Forte, I really don't think you need to send your cousins from Palermo to see me... Yes. ...Yes. ....Yes... NO, thank YOU! Okay, I'll see who I can find. Yes, goodbye."

Mr Dixon looks up and smiles at Denise Shepherd. Denise smiles back.

Yes, he is one of those "nice young men" that grand-mothers love. He has a 'nice' haircut, he **sits up straight**, wears clean white shirts, has a **nine-to-five job**, and probably opens car doors for women. Denise feels sure that when any-body asks him how he is, he always answers, "Very well, thank you," even when it isn't true.

For a long time, she always said "Very well, thank you", too, even when she wasn't. It took her a long time to change that. Perhaps she could help him as well.

"No, I don't want a job working for Mr Forte, whoever he is," she says with a grin.

Without batting an eyelid, Mr Dixon replies, "I don't think that after that call I can think of anybody else for the job. I believe Mr Forte has a big family. Perhaps they have time to work for him. I definitely don't want to see them here!"

With that, to Denise's **amusement**, Mr Dixon drops the notes for Mr Forte into the **wastepaper bin**.

Edward Dixon is surprised at himself. He never does things like that usually, and he doesn't know why he **decided** to do it now. But it was fun and he feels good.

to sit up straight	aufrecht sitzen
nine-to-five job	Bürojob (mit geregelter Arbeitszeit)
without batting an eyelid	ohne mit der Wimper zu zucken
amusement	Unterhaltung, Vergnügen
wastepaper bin	Papierkorb
to decide	sich entscheiden

Exercise 5: Present simple or present progressive?
Unterstreichen Sie die richtige Variante!

1. Mr Dixon talks / *is talking* to a client on the phone right now.

2. George Butler works / is working as a waiter this month.

3. Sandra takes / is taking the bus to work every day.

4. Edward usually is getting up / gets up at 6.30 a.m.

5. At the moment, Denise looks / is looking for a new job.

6. He often walks / is walking his dog in the park.

I must look at the new coffee brand in the tea room, he thinks. Perhaps it has extra caffeine. Then he looks again at the woman in front of him.
The young woman is very beautiful. She has a lovely face, green eyes and long black hair.
"So you weren't thinking about working in a restaurant?" he asks her. He is suddenly **serious**, looking at his notes to see how many different jobs there are on the list. "You seem to be trying out different possibilities..."

serious	ernst
lack of direction	Orientierungslosigkeit

The young woman laughs. "You are more diplomatic than your colleague, Mr Banner."
"Oh?"
"Yes, he thinks that I have a complete **lack of direction**."

"Well, in January you worked for the South Coast Tourist Board. In April you were at a PR agency. In June you worked for Marks & Spencer, then a **building company** and a **dentist**. That is quite a spectrum."

Denise Shepherd smiles but says nothing.

"Nobody **sacked** you," Edward continues. "Each time it was you who decided to leave. Nobody says anything bad about you in the notes. They are sorry that you are no longer working for them and would take you back if you ever **change your mind**."

building company	Bauunternehmen
dentist	Zahnarzt
ϟ to sack sb.	jmd. feuern
to change one's mind	es sich anders überlegen
to work out	*hier:* herausfinden
to frown	die Stirn runzeln
confused	verwirrt
unlikely	unwahrscheinlich

"That's very nice of them."

"That's what my neighbour says to the young man from the Jehovah Witnesses!" says Edward grinning. "Perhaps you can tell me what was wrong with the jobs, so that we can **work out** what you are looking for."

Denise **frowns**. "No. All of the jobs were good."

"But not good enough?"

"No, no, they were all good."

Edward is **confused**. "So why did you leave?"

"Because I learned what I needed to learn and did what I needed to do."

"You're not telling me that you learned all there was to learn at the South Coast Tourist Board in three months, are you?"

Denise Shepherd smiles. "No, you're right. That is a bit **unlikely**, isn't it? But it was time for something new. Don't you ever feel like it is time for a change?"

Exercise 6: Question tags. **Vervollständigen Sie die folgenden Fragen mit Fragenanhängseln!**

1. Denise is looking for a job, *isn't she* ?

2. You like people, ________________________?

3. You haven't stayed long in one job, ________________________?

4. I am a difficult client, ________________________?

5. You will help me, ________________________?

6. Edward doesn't usually laugh so much, ________________________?

"Everyone wants a change from time to time," answers Edward. "But some people need it more than others. I think I am right in saying that you need more change than I do?"

He hopes that Denise Shepherd will smile again, but she doesn't.

"I don't agree with you, Mr Dixon. I think everyone needs to go out and do different things. It is very important. There are too many people who do the same thing day after day, year after year, until they die. And why? Because they think that that is how their life has to be. They don't stop and ask themselves if they want to do something different."

Now Edward feels a bit **annoyed**. "That is too simple," he replies. "Lots of people have **responsibilities**, which means

annoyed	verärgert
responsibilities *pl*	*hier:* Verpflichtungen

they have to do jobs that are very routine. They just have to get on with things. That is how they pay the **bills**, buy clothes for their children and put food on the table."

bill	Rechnung
to tap	klopfen, tippen
on time	pünktlich, rechtzeitig
increasingly	zunehmend
uncomfortable	unwohl
to interrupt	unterbrechen
teaspoon	Teelöffel

Edward is in his element. Routine is his favourite hobby. He **taps** his pencil on his desk as he continues. "Routine can be a very positive thing, from cleaning your teeth before you go to bed to coming to work **on time** every day. Or do you think that people going to work every day is something we need to change?"

Denise Shepherd looks amused. "No, Mr Dixon, I don't. But just because somebody goes to work every day doesn't mean they are not doing different things. Some people find new possibilities in the company, others outside the company."

The young woman looks Edward straight in the eyes. "I am talking about those people who see routine as a sort of compass for life."

"I'm not sure I understand what you mean," Edward replies, feeling **increasingly uncomfortable**. This interview is not going well at all. But before he can **interrupt** her, Miss Shepherd continues. "There are people who think it is important to get up at 6 a.m. every morning. They always follow the same routine. They have a shower and put on a clean white shirt. They take the dog for a walk before breakfast. They drink a cup of tea and always eat cornflakes with milk and two **teaspoons** of sugar, followed by toast with butter and marmalade. Then they clean their teeth, put on a jacket and, at 7.30 a.m., take the dog to the neighbour. Then they get on their bike and ride to work. This fixed routine carries on through the day into the evening and the next day, and the next year, and so life goes by. Suddenly life is over, and the person realizes he or she did not even go down to the beach to go on the rollercoaster."

Exercise 7: Unscramble the text. **Lesen Sie weiter und bringen Sie die Sätze in die richtige Reihenfolge!**

☐ **a)** "And what is wrong with that?"

☐ **b)** Then he almost shouts.

☐ **c)** "Yes," answers Miss Shepherd, "I know. It becomes like a religion. Something to hold on to."

☐ **d)** "Some people find routine very important."

☐ **e)** For a couple of seconds, Edward cannot say anything.

Edward is silent again. Miss Shepherd just described his own morning routine exactly. Now that is weird! And it is true: he has never been on a rollercoaster.

printing company	Druckerei
advertising department	Werbeabteilung
to replace sb.	jmd. ersetzen

"Perhaps we should concentrate on the job we have here for you. There is a small **printing company** that is looking for someone for their **advertising department**. Like the other jobs, it is for six months. But that shouldn't be a problem..."
Miss Shepherd nods. "No, that isn't a problem. Anyway, the woman I am **replacing** has family problems, I believe. But I don't think she will need six months before she comes back. The company is in Portslade, isn't it?"

"Yes, did Mr Rochester or Mr Banner tell you about the job?" asks Edward, totally confused.

"No."

"Then how do you...?"

to mutter	murmeln
in fact	*hier:* sogar

Miss Shepherd is already standing up. She is holding out her hand to take the information sheet from Edward.

"You don't need to phone and arrange an interview. It is on my way home. I'll go in and see if they have time to see me."

"But...," Edward **mutters**.

"I'll ring you when I get the job."

And then she leaves.

Edward puts his hand on the back of his head. "*When* I get the job," he mutters. "When I get the job, not even *if* I get the job." Something tells him that she will get the job. **In fact**, he is sure about it.

Exercise 8: Tell or say? Unterstreichen Sie die richtige Variante!

1. Edward asks her to say / *tell* him what is wrong with the job.
2. She says / tells that she has no problems with the job.
3. She says / tells the printing company that she wants the job.
4. "You've got the job," says / tells the HR manager.
5. Tell / Say him not to be so sure about the importance of routine.

About an hour later, while Edward is talking to a young **carpenter**, his telephone rings. It is the manager of the printing company. He really likes Denise Shepherd and she is going to start working for them on Thursday. Edward phones Mr Rochester to tell him that Denise Shepherd already has another job.

carpenter	Schreiner
to hang up	auflegen
brave	mutig, tapfer
to be lucky	Glück haben
bench	Bank

"Hard to believe," is all Mr Rochester says before he **hangs up**.

The rest of the day continues more normally. Edward and Sandra drink a coffee together in the kitchen and Edward tells his colleague about Denise Shepherd.

"She not only sounds a little weird; she sounds very **brave** (i)," says Sandra smiling.

Es gibt im Deutschen und Englischen viele „falsche Freunde", sogenannte „false friends". Z.B. brave wird oft als Englisch für „brav" missverstanden. Es bedeutet aber mutig, tapfer. Andere typische Beispiele sind:
actual = ‚eigentlich' und nicht ‚aktuell'
become = ‚werden' und nicht ‚bekommen'
eventually = ‚endlich' und nicht ‚eventuell'
also = ‚auch' und nicht ‚also'

"Brave?" Edward does not know what she means.

Sandra grins. "She told you 'some people' make a religion out of routine. Well, anyone who says anything against routine when you are listening is **lucky** to leave the room alive."

Edward has to laugh. "I'm not that bad."

Sandra puts down her mug and goes to the door. "Yes, you are!"

The next person on Edward's list is a 40-year-old woman

called Barbara Partridge. She has worked as a secretary for twenty years for the same man. The company is not doing very well, so she and her boss have to leave.
"I'm sorry to hear that," says Edward. "You'll be happy to hear that there are a lot of people looking for secretaries. It will be easy to find you another job."
"Nothing too routine, I hope," the secretary replies. "My last job was only routine. I think I need a change."
There is a snort from Sandra's table, which Edward ignores.
"A bit of routine can be good," he says quite loudly.
There is another loud snort from Sandra's table.

Exercise 9: True or false? Welche Aussagen zur Geschichte sind korrekt? Kreuzen Sie an!

1. The manager of the printing company likes Denise. ❐
2. The advertising department needs someone for one year. ❐
3. Sandra thinks Denise is very brave. ❐
4. Edward feels sure that Denise will get the job. ❐
5. Barbara Partridge has been a secretary for 10 years. ❐
6. Ms Partridge would like a job with more routine. ❐

That evening, Edward walks around the park with Minnie. As always, he turns into the rhododendron alley and right at the big oak tree. There is a **bench** under the oak tree and Edward sits down to think. He comes here quite often – since his father died in a car **accident**. At first he came here to get away[i] from his mother. She was so unhappy. She tried to be happy for Edward, but he saw how sad she was. It was his mother who showed him how important routine was to **get through** each day. She did everything in a very organized way. She showed him how to do everything in the house when she could no longer do anything because she was so ill. One day, soon after his eighteenth birthday, she died.

accident	Unfall
↯ **to get through sth.**	etw. durchstehen
lonely	einsam
to stroke	streicheln
to wag one's tail	mit dem Schwanz wedeln

Suddenly he was completely on his own. His routine helped him to get through the months that followed. Until it became a part of him. It helped him when his wife left him for one of his friends. And yes, it gives his life direction.

He can no longer remember exactly why he married Mary, but he thinks that they were both **lonely**. He is happy that she is happy with Barry, and especially that she does not want to come back. She now lives in Great Yarmouth, a long way from Brighton, which is good.

Minnie comes and sits next to him and puts her head on his knees.

"You're a good girl," he says, **stroking** her head. Why don't we do something different today and walk down to the beach this evening? I'd love to have an ice-cream. What do you think?"

Minnie **wags her tail.** A longer walk? Great idea!

Phrasal verbs mit **to get**
to get away (entkommen)
to get on with sth. (weitermachen)
to get on with sb. (sich mit jmd. gut verstehen)
to get up (aufstehen)

Exercise 10: Crossword puzzle. Lösen Sie das Kreuzworträtsel! Fast alle Jobs kommen in der Geschichte vor.

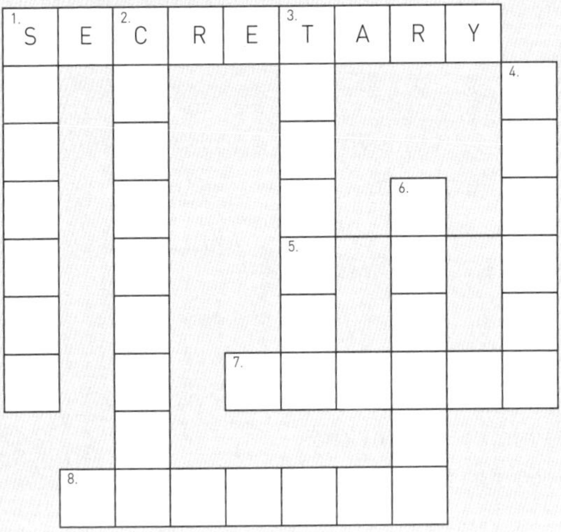

Across

1. someone who organizes things at the office and types letters to clients

5. Edward is a kind man; he has a good ________.

7. Charles Dickens was a ________.

8. a person who works on the machines that print books

Down

1. a person studying at university

2. a person who makes things out of wood

3. a person you can learn things from

4. You go to this person when you are ill.

6. a man who brings your food and drink in a restaurant

Two months later, Denise Shepherd phones to say that she needs another job. The day before her **appointment** Edward contacts the printing company. He is surprised when the manager himself comes to the phone.
"Mr Dixon?"
"Yes!"
"My secretary tells me you are phoning from the Job Centre about Denise Shepherd..."
"Yes, I want to ask how things went, if there was a problem..."
"Problem? No! There was no problem. Denise Shepherd was fantastic. She **worked magic**, both for our advertising department and for Angela Brown."
"Angela Brown?"
"Angela Brown, our advertising manager, lost her husband at Christmas. She was **devastated**. She wanted to leave the company. She felt she couldn't work any longer. We tried, but we didn't know how to help her. Then Denise Shepherd came, and she was wonderful. She wouldn't let Angela stay at home. She said she needed her help, although I don't think she did. She made Angela feel so important in her work and as a person. Denise made her want to live again. That is how important she was for her. Angela is now back at work and that is why Denise Shepherd is no longer here. Denise Shepherd is a great person. If she ever wants to come back here, let me know. I will find or even *make* her a job!"

appointment	Termin
to work magic	zaubern
devastated	am Boden zerstört
curious	neugierig

Edward is **curious**. He phones the other four companies for which Denise worked this year. The story from each company

is almost the same as the one at the printers.
"No new advisor this time, I see," says Denise Shepherd when she sits down opposite him. She is wearing an **eye-catching** red and white dress this time.

eye-catching	auffallend
open-neck (shirt)	offenes Hemd
It certainly does!	*hier:* Auf jeden Fall! Ganz bestimmt!
to beam with pleasure	vor Freude strahlen

"No," Edward smiles. "How are you?"
"Fine. And you?"
"Not bad."
Denise points at Edward's red, **open-neck** shirt. "We are wearing the same colours today, I see."
"Yes, I saw it for sale near Brighton Pier[i] last week. I wanted to have something a bit different for my holiday next month. It makes a change from the white shirt, doesn't it?"

Brighton Palace Pier ist eine Seebrücke, die 1899 eröffnet wurde. Sie ist 525 m lang, nachts hell erleuchtet (mit ca. 67.000 Lichtern) und u.a. bei Touristen sehr beliebt für ihre Achterbahn.

Denise smiles again. "**It certainly does**!"
Edward picks up the notes on his desk and says, "I have a new challenge for you. A doctor who needs a ghostwriter. He has lots of interesting patients ..."
Denise Shepherd's face **beams with pleasure**. "Yes, that does sound interesting!"

A Difficult Run

Kirsten Marsh

Rory und Dominic könnten nicht gegensätzlicher sein: Der schüchterne und introvertierte Rory bewundert Dominic für sein Selbstbewusstsein und die Furchtlosigkeit, mit der er durchs Leben geht. Doch ein Skiurlaub in Kanada könnte dafür sorgen, dass die Rollen neu verteilt werden. Es gibt nur ein Problem: Rorys Höhenangst.

Rorys Leben hält neben Schule und dem Nebenjob in einem Café kaum Aufregendes bereit. Er träumt davon, etwas von der Welt zu sehen und sich endlich mehr zu trauen.

Dominic ist Rorys bester Freund und sehr selbstverliebt. Er stammt aus reichem Hause und gibt gerne damit an.

Madeleine arbeitet im Restaurant des Skigebiets von Lake Louise. Sie ist hilfsbereit und sieht das Gute in jedem Menschen.

After a long week, Rory and his best friend Dominic pick up their rucksacks and quickly leave college. They are both happy that the weekend is here **at last**. It is March and the sun is shining, but it is still quite **chilly**. So the boys are still wearing their coats.

at last	endlich, schließlich
chilly	frisch
excited	aufgeregt, begeistert
to interrupt	unterbrechen
to exclaim	ausrufen
the suburbs *pl*	Vorort, Stadtrand
to save up	(an)sparen

"Hey Rory, do you want to come over to my house to play computer games tomorrow?" asks Dominic. "We can play that new one. Then we can order a pizza and then we..." Dominic likes to talk a lot. He also often gets a bit **excited**, and when he is excited he talks even more – and even faster. Rory **interrupts** him.

Die häufigsten Haustypen in Großbritannien sind:
detached house (Einfamilienhaus)
semi-detached house (Doppelhaushälfte)
terraced house (Reihenhaus)

"No, I'm sorry. I can't. I'm working at Grind My Beans tomorrow," replies Rory. "Boring!" **exclaims** Dominic. Rory looks at the floor, feeling a bit frustrated. He knows that Dominic doesn't need a part-time job because he is financed by the 'Bank of Mum and Dad'.

Rory's family is not rich like Dominic's. Rory lives in a terraced house near the centre of the large town of Stockport. It's nothing like his friend's large detached house[i] in **the suburbs**.

Rory enjoys his life, but he sometimes thinks it isn't very exciting. He has a weekend job in a coffee shop. He is **saving up** the money he **earns** so that he can go to university one day. He really wants to study Geography at university.

to earn	verdienen
probably	wahrscheinlich
customer	Kunde/Kundin
skinny	dürr, mager
baggy	Schlabber-
as usual	wie üblich
surprised	überrascht
to wonder	sich fragen

Rory is tired when he gets home from a long day at work on Saturday. He thinks about getting into bed early. But I'll **probably** just dream about cappuccinos and difficult **customers**, he thinks. He puts on some music to relax and looks at his **skinny** figure in the mirror. Normally he doesn't care that much about the way he looks, but now he thinks it might be time to join a gym. He changes out of his work uniform and into a **baggy** old t-shirt.

His mobile phone rings and he jumps.
"Hello?" says Rory sleepily.
"Hi, Rory. It's me, Dominic. How was work?" Dominic sounds as excited **as** [i] **usual**.

Um im Englischen zwei Dinge miteinander zu vergleichen, verwendet man: **as...as** = „so ... wie"
Feststehende Vergleiche im Englischen sind z.B.:
She is as pretty as a picture.
John is as blind as a bat.
The children are as hungry as wolves.

"It was – " Rory starts to say.
"Actually, stop! I'm not interested! I have the best news ever!"
Rory is **surprised**. He only saw Dominic yesterday and there was no exciting news then.
"Bethany has a broken knee!" Dominic says excitedly. Bethany is Dominic's younger sister. Rory **wonders** how this is good

news: a broken knee sounds **painful**.

painful	schmerzhaft
Easter	Ostern
to invite	einladen

"That means that Bethany can't come on our skiing holiday to Canada at **Easter**, so mum and David say I can **invite** a friend...," says Dominic quickly.

"Great," replies Rory quietly.

Exercise 1: Opposites. Ersetzen Sie die angegebenen Wörter jeweils mit ihrem Gegenteil!

boring   tired   unlucky   skinny   rich   happy

1. Rory and Dominic are both sad *happy* that the weekend is finally here.
2. It was very lucky ________________ to break her knee just before a skiing holiday.
3. Rory looks at his fat ________________ figure in the mirror.
4. Dominic thinks it is exciting ________________ that Rory is going to work the following day.
5. Dominic's family has a large house because they are poor ________________.
6. Rory is feeling lively ________________ after work.

"That's you, you idiot! And you don't have to pay for anything. Just say yes!" exclaims Dominic. There is a moment's silence. "Okay, let me think about it," says Rory. This is not the reaction that Dominic is hoping for.
Rory puts down the phone and suddenly his tiredness is gone. On the one hand, it is a perfect **opportunity**. Rory **gets on well with** Dominic's family and he has time off college and work at Easter. However, there is just one thing stopping him from saying yes: Rory is really **scared of heights.** He doesn't know why. He knows that for some reason he isn't scared of flying; he has flown to Spain with his family a few of times and that was okay. But ski lifts? This is a new **challenge**! Rory never speaks to anybody about his fear of heights because he is the type of person who **keeps his feelings to himself**.

opportunity	Gelegenheit
to get on well with sb.	gut mit jmd. auskommen
to be scared of heights	Höhenangst haben
challenge	Herausforderung
to keep one's feelings to oneself	die Gefühle für sich behalten
factory	Fabrik
to hurt oneself	sich verletzen
to make decisions	Entscheidungen treffen

Rory goes downstairs and tells his mum that Dominic wants him to come on their family holiday to Canada. Rory's Dad is at work; he works nights at a local **factory**. His mum doesn't understand why Rory wants to go skiing, but she is also afraid that he will **hurt himself**. However, she doesn't stop him. Rory is happy to have this freedom and that his mum lets him **make** his own **decisions**.

Rory thinks about Dominic's invitation a lot that evening. He finally decides that it is such a great opportunity, it would be stupid to say no. Later that night Rory sends Dominic a message: 'Yes, I would love to come! Sorry for being so quiet on the phone – long day at work'. Dominic replies **immediately** with lots of smiley faces. He seems very happy that his best friend is coming on holiday with him. Rory stays up watching online videos about skiing until after 3 a.m. He just can't stop watching. He also researches what clothing and **equipment** he needs to buy or **borrow**.

immediately	sofort
equipment	Ausrüstung
to borrow	ausleihen
to pass	*hier:* vorübergehen
to exercise	Sport machen
to worry	sich Sorgen machen
ϟ to whizz down the slopes	die Pisten heruntersausen

Time **passes** really slowly for the next three weeks until the holiday is finally here. Every night Rory watches more videos about skiing and starts to **exercise** to get fit. Of course he doesn't tell Dominic about any of this. Dominic loves skiing and goes on a ski holiday with his family every year. Dominic never **worries** about anything. He will be **whizzing down the slopes** as soon as they get there. Finally the Easter holidays arrive.

Calgary ist die größte kanadische Stadt zwischen Vancouver und Toronto und liegt in unmittelbarer Nähe zu den Rocky Mountains. Die Stadt ist vor allem bekannt für ihre jährlich stattfindende Landwirtschaftsausstellung, die *Calgary Stampede.*

After a twelve hour flight from Manchester to Calgary[i] via Amsterdam, and a bus ride from Calgary to the resort of Lake Louise in the Rocky Mountains, they finally check into their hotel.

Exercise 2: Multiple choice. Welcher Satz ist korrekt? Kreuzen Sie an!

1. ☐ **a)** He is really scared of heights.
   ☐ **b)** He is really scared for heights.

2. ☐ **a)** He gets really well with Dominic's family.
   ☐ **b)** He gets on really well with Dominic's family.

3. ☐ **a)** His mum don't understands why he wants to go.
   ☐ **b)** His mum doesn't understand why he wants to go.

4. ☐ **a)** Rory likes to keep his feelings to himself.
   ☐ **b)** Rory likes to keep his feelings to hisself.

5. ☐ **a)** His Dad is in work on a factory.
   ☐ **b)** His Dad is at work in a factory.

6. ☐ **a)** Dominic is going skiing every year.
   ☐ **b)** Dominic goes skiing every year.

Everybody knows that the Rocky Mountains are beautiful. But the view from the window of his room leaves Rory **speechless**. He can see thousands of **snow-covered** trees, with **jagged** mountains in the distance. It is really beautiful. He knows this type of landscape from his geography lessons, but he is really excited to see it in real life.

Rory can't sleep that night. He can't decide if it's because of excitement or fear. Perhaps both, he thinks.

speechless	sprachlos
snow-covered	mit Schnee bedeckt
jagged	gezackt
to rent	mieten
ski goggles *pl*	Skibrille
to head for sth.	etw. ansteuern, auf etw. zugehen
to lie	lügen
ant	Ameise
chairlift	Sessellift
to show off	angeben

At breakfast the next morning, Dominic is even more excited than usual. He talks non-stop. When they get to the ski area, the sun is just coming up and the sky is blue. It is minus 10 degrees – cold, but a beautiful day. They go to pick up the equipment they have **rented**.

"See you later, Rory!" Dominic says, as soon as they have their boots and skis. He can't wait to be on the slopes. He pulls down his **ski goggles** and **heads for** the lift.

"Will you be okay, Rory?" asks Dominic's mum.

"Yes, fine," Rory **lies**.

"I think I will take some ski lessons," he says. He hopes that he can still book a class.

"Okay, hopefully see you at lunchtime then!" says Dominic's mum as she and her partner ski off.

Rory is alone now. He stares up at the ski hill. The skiers higher up the mountain look like **ants** in the distance.

I don't have enough money for many ski lessons, he thinks. But why take lessons if I can't ride the **chairlift** anyway? Rory stands still for another 15 minutes with these thoughts going around his head.

Some distance away Dominic is trying to ski backwards. He is **showing off** to a group of girls and doesn't see Rory. On the one hand, Rory finds it **embarrassing** when his best friend shows off like that. On the other hand, sometimes he would like to have the same **confidence** and talk to girls in the same way that Dominic does.

Rory starts to get cold. He goes into the wooden **ski lodge** and buys himself a coffee. It is delicious – much nicer than the coffees that he makes for customers at Grind My Beans. This life seems so different from his life in Stockport. But he can't just sit around drinking coffee for the next week.

Exercise 3: Unscramble the sentences. Bringen Sie die Wörter in die richtige Reihenfolge!

1. The | takes | flight | hours | twelve

   The flight takes twelve hours.

2. views | are | beautiful | The | really

   ____

3. decide | can't | from | excitement | it is | He | fear | if | or

   ____

4. shows | to | Dominic | off | girls

   ____

5. Rory | Dominic | is | confident | not | as | as

   ____

Before he knows it, it is midday. He **avoids** Dominic and his family because he is sure they will ask about his skiing lessons. He can't tell them about his fear. So he **continues** walking around the bottom of the slope. "You are being so silly," he tells himself. "You know the lift is completely safe. Just do it!"

embarrassing	peinlich
confidence	Selbstvertrauen
ski lodge	Skihütte
to avoid	vermeiden
to continue	weitermachen, fortfahren
to copy sb./sth.	jmd./etw. nachmachen
queue	(Warte-) Schlange
to feel sick	übel sein
to fail	versagen, scheitern
snowplough position	im Pflug
to slide	rutschen

Rory suddenly picks up his skis and walks over to the chairlift. He has decided: he is going to do it! He watches how other people are putting on their skis and **copies** them. In front of him in the **queue** are a happy couple who are smiling and laughing. Rory **feels sick**. When he gets to the front of the queue he realizes that he simply can't do it. Rory's fear wins – and he has **failed**. He is so frustrated with himself. He goes back into the lodge and orders another coffee.

The caffeine gives him the kick he needs. He has to do *something*. So he picks up his skis and heads for the beginners slope. There is a small ski lift for children but Rory decides to walk up. Three-year-old children are skiing down the slope, whizzing past him as he walks up. How hard can it be if they can do it? Rory asks himself. When he gets to the top of the small hill, he stands in a **snowplough position** and slowly **slides** down to the bottom. He tries it again – and then again.

And each time he gets a little better. **Even though** he doesn't go fast, it feels good. At last he is learning how to ski, and this makes him **proud**.

even though	obwohl
proud	stolz
jealous	eifersüchtig
stool	Hocker
woolly	aus Wolle
familiar	vertraut, bekannt

Rory is very tired at the end of the day when he meets Dominic and his family for dinner, but it is a good kind of tired.
"How was your day, Rory?" asks Dominic. "I wonder why we didn't see you at all...," he continues.
Rory starts to answer, but soon his friend interrupts him because he is more interested in talking about his own day.
"I went right up to the top. The snow was great. I skied down sooooo fast. It was fantastic. There were lots of lovely Canadian girls up there, too. Look, here are the photos. You must come out there with me..."
Dominic can't stop talking about himself and his day. Rory feels a bit **jealous**, but he is also happy that Dominic is having a good time.

They go back to the hotel to shower and get changed, and then Rory, Dominic and his parents all go out for a meal. After drinking so many coffees but not eating anything, Rory is really hungry. They go to a local restaurant.

"Eh" ist ein typisches kanadisches Slang-Wort. Am Ende eines Satzes benutzt, bedeutet der Ausdruck soviel wie „Nicht wahr?".

The group find a table, and Rory goes over to the bar to order some drinks.
"You're the one who couldn't get enough coffee today, eh[i]?" says a young lady sitting on a bar **stool**. She has long brown

hair and a strong Canadian accent. The green **woolly** hat which she is wearing is almost the same colour as her eyes.
"Ummm, uhhh, yes," stutters Rory.

Exercise 4: Word search. **In diesem Gitternetz sind neun Adjektive versteckt. Finden Sie sie!**

F	A	S	T	J	T	A	S
A	S	I	I	E	L	G	T
N	I	L	H	A	P	P	Y
T	L	S	I	L	L	Y	W
A	A	O	N	O	A	D	G
S	P	R	O	U	D	K	R
T	S	A	F	S	A	F	E
I	L	E	B	A	L	R	A
C	H	U	N	G	R	Y	T

"I'm Madeleine, nice to meet you." Madeline shakes Rory's hand and he thinks that she looks **familiar**.
"It seems you love drinking coffee more than skiing!" she laughs. "Or do you just like being inside more than outside?"
He then suddenly remembers where he knows her from: she is the waitress who serves coffee in the lodge.
Rory looks back at the table where Dominic is busy showing David the photos from his head-cam.

"The thing is...," says Rory quietly, "I have nothing else to do. I'm... erm... scared of heights, so I can't take the chairlift," he continues.
He has no idea why he is telling a total **stranger** about his fear when he can't even tell his parents or his best friend. But it feels good to say it out loud.

stranger	Fremde
confused	verwirrt
maple leaf	Ahornblatt
breathing	Atmung
convinced	überzeugt
to hold one's breath	die Luft anhalten

"Listen, it's my day off tomorrow. If you meet me at the lodge at 10 a.m., I can show you how to do it," she says.
"Okay," says Rory. He has no idea why she wants to help him, but back at the table he doesn't have time to think about it. Dominic continues to talk about his day and show the statistics from his smart watch as they all eat their burgers and fries.

The next morning Rory arrives at the lodge at 10 a.m. He feels really nervous and is happy to see Madeleine walking towards him with her skis over her shoulder.
"Hi Madeleine!" he says enthusiastically.
"Hi Rory, nice toque!" says Madeleine.
Rory looks **confused**. Madeleine points to his hat. It is from the ski shop and is red and white with a Canadian **maple leaf** on it. Rory later realizes that the Canadians have different words for some things, and 'toque' was just one of them.

Die Kanadier sind stolz auf ihr kulturelles Erbe und ihre sprachliche Vielfalt. Es gibt einige Wörter, die sich vom Britischen oder Amerikanischen Englisch unterscheiden – „toque" zum Beispiel ist kanadischer Slang für eine Wollmütze.

Exercise 5: Choose the right word. Lesen Sie weiter und unterstreichen Sie das richtige Wort!

Madeleine **1.** wants to / want to get Rory onto the slopes.

"Look, I go up **2.** there / their hundreds of times a year and I promise you **3.** its / it's completely **4.** save / safe," says Madeleine.

"I keep telling **5.** myself / me that, but my fear is not rational," replies Rory.

"Okay, I **6.** am understanding / understand. You **7.** need / needs to concentrate on your **breathing**," says Madeleine.

"How **8.** I do / do I do that?" Rory doesn't sound **convinced**.

"Breathe in through your nose. Now **hold your breath** and count to five," she says. He does what she says.
"Now breathe out through the mouth," she continues.
She spends the next ten minutes showing him how to use breathing to fight his fear. Rory is surprised how much calmer he already feels. The sick feeling from the day before is almost gone.
"I think it's working. How do you know how to do this?" asks Rory.
"I do a lot of yoga." Madeleine replies.
Madeleine then skis over to join the queue for the ski lift and Rory follows her. She continues to do the breathing exercises

with him as they move forward in the queue.
He can't **back out** this time. He has no **choice**; he will have to get on the chairlift with Madeleine! She smiles at the lift attendant and asks him to slow down the chairlift so that Rory can get on. He gets on the lift easily, sits down and looks **straight ahead**.
Madeleine says, "Watch out for bears on the way down!"
Rory is shocked. Bears? **Chasing** him down the slope?
"**Only joking!**" she laughs. "The bears are normally asleep during the winter." Rory feels a bit silly.

Madeleine keeps **distracting** him with funny stories, and before he knows it, they get to the top of the chairlift. He realizes that he didn't look down once. Madeleine lifts up the **bar** and they both jump off the lift together. So the breathing techniques and her strategy to distract him worked! He is so happy and thankful to Madeleine.

Exercise 6: Prepositions. Ergänzen Sie den Text mit den Präpositionen!

through ~~at~~ during with next to to

1. Madeleine smiles __*at*__ the lift attendant.
2. Rory breathes in __________ the nose and out __________ the mouth.
3. Rory sits __________ Madeleine on the lift.
4. The bears are asleep __________ winter.
5. Madeleine distracted him __________ funny stories.
6. She tells him to count __________ five.

Madeleine takes him down a green **run** from the top of the hill. She explains to him that green runs are the easiest type of run. He continues to **practice** his snowplough turns.
"You've got a good technique," she says. "I can't believe this is your first time skiing".
"I watched a lot of videos online," he replies.

to back out	abspringen, aussteigen
choice	Wahl
straight ahead	geradeaus
to chase	(hinterher) jagen
ϟ Only joking!	Nur ein Scherz!
to distract	ablenken
bar	*hier:* (Lift-) Stange
to work	*hier:* funktionieren
run	*hier:* Abfahrt, Piste
to practice	üben
to enjoy	genießen
to ache	wehtun, schmerzen

They ski a few more runs together. Each time Rory goes up on the lift he does the breathing exercises. He still doesn't **enjoy** it, but every time it gets easier and easier.
By midday his legs are starting to **ache**. He feels bad that Madeleine is using so much of her time to help him.
"You can go off and see your friends if you want. You really don't have to stay with me. I'm just slowing you down," he says.
"Don't be silly! [i] Let's go for lunch," she says.

Die englische Floskel "Don't be silly!" wird sehr häufig verwendet und bedeutet soviel wie „Sei nicht albern!". Man verwendet sie z.B., wenn sich jmd. für etwas entschuldigt, für das er/sie sich nicht entschuldigen müsste.

They go to the lodge. A friend of hers is working and gives them a free lunch.
"We'll have two portions of poutine and two coffees please," she says.

The waitress serves them with two plates of **chips**, **gravy** and cheese. Rory thinks it looks a bit **strange**, but he says nothing because he doesn't want to be **impolite**. They sit down to eat, and he is surprised that it is actually very **tasty**.

chips (Br.E.)	Pommes
gravy	Bratensoße
strange	seltsam
impolite	unhöflich
tasty	lecker
impressed	beeindruckt
to encourage	ermutigen

"That tastes really good," says Rory.
"It's a Canadian speciality!" replies Madeleine.

After their meal Madeleine takes him down a different slope. She is so **impressed** with his skiing that she **encourages** him to go down a blue run. This is harder than the green run and to begin with Rory finds it is difficult to turn. He tries to turn, but his skis won't move where he wants them to. It is the first time that Rory falls over and his skis fall off. He feels very embarrassed but Madeleine comes over immediately and helps him. Then he stands up and slowly continues down the rest of the slope. She encourages him to try the same run again. At first he is nervous, but he skis perfectly the second time. He feels so good and so free – like never before. Usually he worries about a lot of things – his exams, his job, his friends... But when he is skiing he seems to forget about everything. He feels completely free.
"This is amazing," he shouts to Madeleine as he is whizzing down the blue run.
"You're awesome," she replies. He doesn't know what to say to that, so he doesn't say anything.
They continue skiing all afternoon. Rory thinks back to the day before and can't believe how much better he is feeling.

Exercise 7: Questions about the text. Beantworten Sie die Fragen zum Text. Schreiben Sie ganze Sätze!

1. What do Rory and Madeleine eat for lunch?

   They eat poutine, which is chips, gravy and cheese.

2. Which ski runs are the easiest type of run?

   ____

3. What does Madeleine think about Rory's skiing?

   ____

4. How does Rory feel when he falls over for the first time?

   ____

5. How does Rory learn about skiing before the holiday?

   ____

6. Why does Rory love skiing?

   ____

The following day Madeleine has to work again, so Rory practices on the slopes that Madeleine showed him the day before. He goes into the lodge for a break and Madeleine gives him a free coffee. She is busy at work so she doesn't have time to talk, but she gives him a warm smile and tells him to enjoy the rest of his day.

At the end of the morning he sits at the top of the mountain and looks down below at the snow-covered trees, **frozen** lakes and blue sky. He can't believe how much he is enjoying it.

frozen	(ein)gefroren
to introduce	vorstellen

Dominic, his mum and David ski up behind him and interrupt his thoughts.
"Aren't you having any lessons today, Rory?" Dominic's mum asks.
"No, I don't think I need them anymore!" says Rory.
"Are you having a good day?" Rory asks them.
"Brilliant!" exclaims Dominic.
"We can't keep up with him!" says his mum, pointing at Dominic, who is already starting to ski down the slope.
"My knees are aching! We're getting too old for this!" says David.
They all ski down together. Dominic shows off, as usual, but when they get to the bottom Rory can see that Dominic is impressed with how well Rory can already ski.
"Do you want to ski with me tomorrow?" asks Dominic. "I'll show you a couple of good runs and a jump that I did this morning. It'll be much better than skiing with my parents," he continues. Rory isn't sure that he is ready for jumps yet. He has only been skiing for two days!

Rory and Dominic spend the next few days together. They get along really well. At home they usually stay inside playing computer games all day, so it feels good to be outdoors in the fresh mountain air. In the evenings they sometimes play cards with Madeleine. She **introduces** them to some of her friends.

Exercise 8: Translation quiz. Übersetzen Sie und finden Sie das Lösungswort!

1. vorstellen _ _ _ _ ☐ _ _ _ _

2. Berg _ _ ☐ _ _ _ _ _

3. unterbrechen _ _ ☐ _ _ _ _ _ _

4. verbringen _ _ _ _ ☐

5. genießen _ _ _ ☐ _

6. (ein)gefroren _ _ ☐ _ _ _

7. üben _ ☐ _ _ _ _ _ _

8. beeindruckt _ _ _ _ _ _ _ ☐ _ _

Lösung: ☐ ☐ ☐ ☐ ☐ ☐ ☐ ☐

On the last day of the holiday Madeleine has another day off, so they all decide to spend the day skiing together. Later in the morning Madeleine sees one of her friends, Tina, and they all ski together for a couple of runs. Again, Dominic starts showing off.

"I think I could be in the next Winter Olympics!" says Dominic.

"Yes, I'm sure you could!" replies Madeleine jokingly.

Dominic skis down the slope as fast as he can. He is even faster than the days before. Rory can't keep up with him.

Dominic then goes over a small jump at the side of the run and flies up into the air. He lands on his back and then slides down the hill on his **bum**. His skis don't fall off and so it looks very funny. Finally a tree stops him. Everybody laughs. "Ouch!" exclaims Dominic. "Are you hurt?" asks Tina, but Madeleine and Rory can't stop laughing.

⚡ **bum**	Hintern, Po
to brush off	abklopfen
angry	wütend, verärgert

"Don't worry, I'm okay!" says Dominic. Rory takes out his mobile phone and takes a photograph of Dominic.
"I think it was just a bit of ice... it is really cold today!" Dominic says, looking embarrassed. He soon gets up, **brushes off** the snow and continues down the slope. He is slower this time so Rory can ski next to him.
"I have a great photo of you!" says Rory.
"Don't show it to anyone!" Dominic shouts back at Rory. He sounds quite **angry**.

Exercise 9: Opposites. **Wie lautet das Gegenteil? Ordnen Sie zu!**

1. ☐ continue	a) ugly
2. ☐ beautiful	b) serious
3. ☐ angry	c) boring
4. ☐ interesting	d) stop
5. ☐ joking	e) calm

On the last afternoon, Madeleine decides to show the boys her favourite run.
"Do you think you're ready for a black diamond run now?" she asks as they ride up the chairlift.
"Isn't that the hardest type of run?" asks Rory nervously.
"Yes, but I think you're ready for it!" says Madeleine in her usual optimistic way.
"Erm, I'm not sure," Rory says, at the same time as Dominic shouts "definitely!"
When they get to the top of the slope, Rory is shocked to see how **steep** it is. And he sees another skier sliding on a **patch** of ice as he skis down.
"Come on!" Madeleine says.
Oh no! thinks Rory. I can just see myself going back to college with a broken leg. Madeleine goes down first. Rory follows Madeleine down the slope and concentrates hard. He is slow at first, but he feels in control.
And he isn't scared.
"Can you **keep up** with me?" shouts Dominic as he skis past. Rory sees this as a challenge and **speeds up**.
"Of course I can!" shouts Rory. The feeling is great. And when he gets to the bottom of the slope Rory feels very proud of himself.
"Wow, great work!" says Madeleine as they take off their skis.

steep	steil
patch	Fleck, Stelle
to keep up with sb.	mit jmd. mithalten
to speed up	schneller werden; beschleunigen

On their last night together they all go out for dinner at the restaurant where Rory first met Madeleine. They start to talk about the past week.

Exercise 10: Verb forms. Lesen Sie weiter und setzen Sie die korrekte Verbform ein!

"I'm really impressed how you **1.** overcome *overcame* your fear. You should be so proud!" exclaims Madeleine.

"What fear?" asks Dominic. Rory **2.** feel ______________ his face going the colour of a tomato.

"His fear of heights!" **3.** say ______________ Madeleine. She then suddenly stops talking as she realizes that Dominic **4.** not know ______________ about his friend's fear.

"Oh," says Dominic to Rory. "Why didn't you tell me?" He doesn't laugh or **make a big deal out of** it. Rory relaxes. He **5.** not expect ______________ this reaction from his best friend.

As soon as Madeleine goes to the toilet, Dominic starts to **6.** ask ______________ questions about her.

"So, is it official then? Is she your girlfriend?"
"Why do you think that?" Rory asks.
"Isn't it **obvious**?" says Dominic.
They talk some more, and Rory suddenly starts to wonder about his new friend, Madeleine. Why does she take the time to help him? Is she just a friendly person? Does she like him in another way? A thousand questions run through his mind.

When Madeleine comes back she tries to convince Rory to come out to do a ski season with her after he finishes sixth-form college[i] and before he goes to university.

> In Großbritannien besuchen die meisten Schüler das sogenannte **sixth form college**, eine Oberstufe für Schüler zwischen 16-19 Jahren, die sie für den Abschluss (A Levels) vorbereitet.

"It's so great out here," says Madeleine. "Lots of people from all over the world come out here and work for a season. I've got friends from Australia, the UK, Japan... everywhere. There are lots of jobs. You could work on a ski lift! Or if not, then in the lodge. You could do it before you go off to university."
"I'll think about it," says Rory.

After they finish eating, Dominic, his mum and David leave the restaurant **ahead of** Rory, leaving him alone with Madeleine for a minute. Madeleine hugs Rory goodbye, and puts a small present in his hand. It is a toy grizzly bear. He remembers their first ride up the ski lift together. He hugs her **tightly**.

On the plane on the way home, Rory sits by the window. Madeleine's words give him hope for a more exciting future. He suddenly realizes how small he is and how big everything else is. He feels much **braver** now than he did before, and he is sure that he is going to see a lot more of this big world. Perhaps he will see Canada again, and maybe even Madeleine, too.

ϟ **to make a big deal out of sth.**	eine große Sache aus etw. machen
obvious	offensichtlich
ahead of sb.	vor jmd.
tightly	fest
brave	mutig, tapfer

Final Test
Answers
Glossary
List of Exercises

Final Test

Exercise 1: Adjectives and adverbs. **Unterstreichen Sie die richtige Variante!**

1. Fresh / Freshly baked bread tastes wonderful.
2. Rosemary is a very patient / patiently woman.
3. He shuffled very slow / slowly through the door?
4. Please stop laughing and take this serious / seriously.
5. I can't believe he ate all the cake. He is so greedy / greedily.

Exercise 2: Translation quiz. **Übersetzen Sie die Wörter ins Englische und enträtseln Sie das Lösungswort!**

1. bequem ☐ _ _ _ _ _ _ _ _ _ _
2. egoistisch _ _ _ _ _ _ ☐
3. Kleiderschrank _ ☐ _ _ _ _ _ _
4. in Rente _ _ _ _ ☐ _ _
5. erfolgreich _ _ _ _ _ _ _ _ _ ☐
6. Krawatte _ _ ☐
7. Ehemann _ _ ☐ _ _ _ _

Lösungswort: ☐ ☐ ☐ ☐ ☐ ☐ ☐

Exercise 3: Odd one out. Finden Sie das Wort, das nicht in die Reihe passt!

1. calm excited surprised amazed angry
2. cow dog deer vehicle hare
3. bread rolls porridge rope soup sandwich
4. eventually at last finally in the end soon

Exercise 4: Fill in the blanks. Enträtseln Sie die Wortketten!

1. disappe ☐☐ ms
2. adventu ☐☐ mote
3. famili ☐☐ rive
4. lo ☐☐ eep

Exercise 5: True or false? Welche Aussagen aus *A Difficult Run* sind korrekt? Markieren Sie mit richtig ✓ oder falsch — und korrigieren Sie!

1. Rory has a part-time job in Stockport. ☐
2. Rory is saving up to study History at university. ☐
3. Madeleine works as a ski instructor. ☐
4. Rory is wearing a hat with the Union Jack on it to show he is British. ☐

Answers

Till Death Us Do Part

Exercise 1: **1.** much **2.** many **3.** many **4.** much **5.** many

Exercise 2: **1.** e **2.** c **3.** a **4.** b **5.** d

Exercise 3: **1.** rings **2.** forget **3.** tell **4.** lost **5.** did (you) find **6.** took **7.** look **8.** am

Exercise 4: **1.** b **2.** a **3.** b **4.** a **5.** a

Exercise 5: **1.** d **2.** a **3.** e **4.** b **5.** c

Exercise 6: **1.** You know she is her best friend.
2. He starts eating it. **3.** They talk about them. **4.** We are going to a restaurant.
5. I hope he gives us a good table.

Exercise 7: **1.** Charles doesn't want Rosemary to listen to other people.
2. He isn't happy about the spa hotel in Bath.
3. She can't understand why he is upset.
4. I'm not going to let him order me about.
5. I don't need time for myself.

Exercise 8: **1.** herself **2.** himself **3.** myself **4.** yourself **5.** themselves

Exercise 9: **1.** reminds **2.** remembers **3.** remember **4.** reminds **5.** remind

Highland Heroes

Exercise 1: **1.** porridge **2.** kisses **3.** visitor **4.** tired **5.** rest

Exercise 2: **1.** bakery **2.** village, rolls **3.** hiker **4.** queue, decide **5.** grabs

Exercise 3: **1.** false (They live outside the village.) **2.** false (Morag has long, ginger hair.) **3.** false (The policeman is wearing a black uniform.) **4.** true **5.** false (It is spring.)

Exercise 4: **1.** c **2.** a **3.** e **4.** b **5.** d

Exercise 5: **1.** we'll **2.** that's **3.** they're **4.** can't **5.** they've

Exercise 6: **1.** a herd of deer **2.** purple **3.** sandwiches **4.** steep and rocky **5.** wind and birds

Exercise 7: **1.** Do you think **2.** is just following **3.** I hope not **4.** Morag's **5.** I'm/ I am **6.** we will find **7.** talk to the small dog **8.** Dougal barks

Exercise 8:

W	A	T	E	R	P	R	O	O	F
R	N	T	A	O	I	O	N	L	I
U	G	B	H	P	E	P	U	N	R
C	R	E	S	C	U	E	I	F	S
K	R	A	E	Z	U	N	E	R	T
S	W	E	A	T	E	R	O	A	A
A	J	G	R	V	P	E	S	N	I
C	J	A	C	K	E	T	M	K	D
K	U	T	H	S	T	R	E	A	K
O	I	N	J	U	R	E	D	G	I
Y	O	R	B	L	A	N	K	E	T

Exercise 9: **1.** follows, followed **2.** carries, carried **3.** greets, greeted **4.** touches, touched **5.** tries, tried

Exercise 10: **1.** them **2.** it **3.** her **4.** him **5.** us

Time for a Change

Exercise 1: **1.** at **2.** by **3.** at **4.** in **5.** on **6.** on

Exercise 2: **1.** is, was **2.** says, said **3.** replies, replied **4.** continues, continued **5.** shakes, shook **6.** makes, made

Exercise 3: **1.** office **2.** plate **3.** desk **4.** neighbour **5.** meets **6.** angry

Exercise 4: **1.** nice **2.** weird **3.** bored **4.** quiet **5.** broad

Exercise 5: **1.** is talking **2.** is working **3.** takes **4.** gets up **5.** is looking **6.** walks

Exercise 6: **1.** isn't she? **2.** don't you? **3.** have you? **4.** aren't I? **5.** won't you? **6.** does he?

Exercise 7: **1.** e **2.** b **3.** a **4.** d **5.** c

Exercise 8: **1.** tell **2.** says **3.** tells **4.** says **5.** tell

Exercise 9: **1.** true **2.** false (They need someone for six months.) **3.** true **4.** true **5.** false (She has been a secretary for the last 20 years.) **6.** false (Her last job was only routine; now she would like a change.)

Exercise 10:

1. S	E	2. C	R	E	3. T	A	R	Y	
T		A			E				4. D
U		R			A				O
D		P			C		6. W		C
E		E			5. H		A		T
N		N			E		I		O
T		T		7. W	R	I	T	E	R
		E					E		
	8. P	R	I	N	T	E	R		

A Difficult Run

Exercise 1: **1.** happy **2.** unlucky **3.** skinny **4.** boring **5.** rich **6.** tired

Exercise 2: **1.** a **2.** b **3.** b **4.** a **5.** b **6.** b

Exercise 3: **1.** The flight takes twelve hours. **2.** The views are really beautiful. **3.** He can't decide if it is from excitement or fear. **4.** Dominic shows off to girls. **5.** Rory is not as confident as Dominic.

Exercise 4:

F	A	S	T	J	T	A	S
A	S	I	I	E	L	G	T
N	I	L	H	A	P	P	Y
T	L	S	I	L	L	Y	W
A	A	O	N	O	A	D	G
S	P	R	O	U	D	K	R
T	S	A	F	S	A	F	E
I	L	E	B	A	L	R	A
C	H	U	N	G	R	Y	T

Exercise 5: **1.** wants to **2.** there **3.** it's **4.** safe **5.** myself **6.** understand **7.** need **8.** How do I do that?

Exercise 6: **1.** at **2.** through **3.** next to **4.** during **5.** with **6.** to

Exercise 7: **1.** They eat poutine, which is chips, gravy and cheese. **2.** The green runs are the easiest. **3.** She is impressed with his skiing./ She can't believe this is his first time skiing. **4.** He feels embarrassed. **5.** He watches videos online. **6.** He forgets about his worries. He feels free like never before.

Exercise 8: **1.** introduce **2.** mountain **3.** interrupt **4.** spend **5.** enjoy **6.** frozen **7.** practise **8.** impressed
Lösung: outdoors

Exercise 9: **1.** d **2.** a **3.** e **4.** c **5.** b

Exercise 10: **1.** overcame **2.** feels **3.** says **4.** doesn't know **5.** didn't expect **6.** ask

Final Test

Exercise 1: **1.** freshly **2.** patient **3.** slowly **4.** seriously **5.** greedy

Exercise 2: **1.** comfortable **2.** selfish **3.** wardrobe **4.** retired **5.** successful **6.** tie **7.** husband
Lösung: Charles

Exercise 3: **1.** calm **2.** vehicle **3.** rope **4.** soon

Exercise 4: **1.** disappear/arms **2.** adventure/remote **3.** familiar/arrive **4.** lost/steep

Exercise 5: **1.** true **2.** false (He wants to study Geography at university.) **3.** false (She works in the ski lodge.) **4.** false (He is wearing a hat with the Canadian maple leaf on it.)

Glossary

ϟ = umgangssprachlich
pl = Plural

accident	Unfall
to ache	wehtun, schmerzen
actually	eigentlich
adventure	Abenteuer
advertising department	Werbeabteilung
advisor	Berater/in
ahead of sb.	vor jmd.
to aim at sth.	auf etw. (ab)zielen
air ambulance	Luftrettungsdienst
almost ready	fast fertig
although	obwohl
amazed	erstaunt
amusement	Unterhaltung, Vergnügen
angle	Winkel
angry (angrily)	wütend, verärgert
annoyed	verärgert
ant	Ameise
antlers *pl*	Geweih
to appear	erscheinen, auftauchen
appointment	Termin
to arrive	ankommen
as soon as	sobald
as usual	wie üblich
at last	endlich, schließlich
at least	mindestens, zumindest
attention	Aufmerksamkeit
to avoid	vermeiden
to back out	abspringen, aussteigen
back page	Rückseite (des Blatts)
to be in a bad mood	schlecht gelaunt sein
baggy	Schlabber-
bar	*hier:* (Lift-)Stange
barely conscious	kaum bei Bewusstsein
to bark	bellen

to beam with pleasure	vor Freude strahlen
to become (became, become)	werden
to belong to sb.	jmd. gehören
bench	Bank
beside	neben
bill	Rechnung
biscuit	Keks
bite	Biss(en)
blanket	Decke
blood pressure	Blutdruck
to borrow	ausleihen
brave(ly)	mutig, tapfer
breathing	Atmung
breathless	atemlos
broad	breit
to brush off	abklopfen
bucket	Eimer
building company	Bauunternehmen
ϟ bum	Hintern, Po
to bump	stoßen, aufschlagen
calmly	ruhig, gelassen
to care	sich kümmern, Gedanken machen
carefree	sorglos
careful(ly)	vorsichtig
carpenter	Schreiner
chairlift	Sessellift
challenge	Herausforderung
to change one's mind	es sich anders überlegen
to chase	(hinterher)jagen
chat	Gespräch, Plausch
cheek	Wange
chicken coop	Hühnerstall
chilly	frisch
chips (Br.E.)	Pommes
choice	Wahl
to choose (chose, chosen)	wählen
to chuckle	kichern
collar	*hier:* Halsband
comfortable	bequem
company	Firma
confidence	Selbstvertrauen
confused	verwirrt
to continue to do sth.	weitermachen, fortfahren
convinced	überzeugt
to copy sb./sth.	jmd./etw. nachmachen

counter	Theke, Tresen
to cover	bedecken, abdecken
crowd	(Menschen-)Menge
curious	neugierig
customer	Kunde/Kundin
dear	Liebste/r, Schatz
to decide	sich entscheiden
deer	Reh
degree	Studienabschluss
dentist	Zahnarzt
devastated	am Boden zerstört
diary	*hier:* Terminkalender
dining room	Esszimmer
to disagree	widersprechen, anderer Meinung sein
to disappear	verschwinden
dishwasher	Geschirrspüler
to distract	ablenken
to drop sth.	etw. fallen lassen
to earn	verdienen
Easter	Ostern
embarrassing	peinlich
emergency	Notfall
employee	Angestellte/r
to encourage	ermutigen
to enjoy oneself	Spaß haben
to enjoy	genießen
equipment	Ausrüstung
especially	besonders
even though	obwohl
eventually	endlich, schließlich
to examine	untersuchen
excited	aufgeregt, begeistert
to exclaim	ausrufen
to exercise	Sport machen
to expect	erwarten
to explain	erklären
expression	Ausdruck
eye-catching	auffallend
factory	Fabrik
to fail	versagen, scheitern
familiar	bekannt, vertraut
farmyard	Bauernhof
to feed (fed, fed)	füttern
to feel (felt, felt) sick	übel sein
finally	endlich

first aid kit	Erstehilfekasten
to fit into	hineinpassen
to flatten	*hier:* flach drücken
to frown	die Stirn runzeln
frozen	(ein)gefroren
garage	*hier:* Werkstatt
to gasp	keuchen, schnaufen
gate	Tor
gateau	Torte
gently	sanft, behutsam
to go (went, gone) away	*hier:* verreisen
to get (got, got) on well with sb.	gut mit jmd. auskommen
ϟ to get through sth.	etw. durchstehen
to get worse	schlimmer werden
to giggle	kichern
ginger	*hier:* rothaarig
to give sb. a lick	jmd. ablecken
glad	froh
ϟ Good heavens!	Um Himmels Willen!
GP (general practitioner)	Hausarzt
to grab sth.	greifen, (sich) schnappen
grateful	dankbar
gravy	Bratensoße
Great Dane	Dogge
greedily	gierig
to growl	knurren
habits *pl*	Angewohnheiten
hall	*hier:* Diele
to hang up	auflegen
hare	Hase
to head for sth.	etw. ansteuern, auf etw. zugehen
head	*hier:* Geschäftsführer, Chef
headline	Schlagzeile
headquarters *pl*	*hier:* die Zentrale
health	Gesundheit
heather	Erika (Heidekraut)
herd of deer *pl*	Hirschrudel
hiker	Wanderer
to hold (held, held) one's breath	die Luft anhalten
How about...?	Wie wäre es mit ...?
however	jedoch, allerdings
HR (Human Resources)	Personalabteilung
to humiliate	erniedrigen
to hurt (hurt, hurt) oneself	sich verletzen

hypothermia	Unterkühlung
to imagine	sich vorstellen
immediately	sofort
impatiently	ungeduldig
impolite	unhöflich
the impossible	das Unmögliche
impressed	beeindruckt
in fact	*hier:* sogar
in public	in der Öffentlichkeit
in the distance	in der Ferne
increasingly	zunehmend
independent	unabhängig
injured	verletzt
instead	stattdessen
to interrupt	unterbrechen
to introduce	vorstellen
to invite	einladen
It certainly does!	*hier:* Auf jeden Fall! Ganz bestimmt!
It's up to you	*hier:* Es liegt ganz an Ihnen
jagged	gezackt
jealous	eifersüchtig
job seeker	Arbeitssuchender
to jump	*hier:* zusammenzucken
to keep (kept, kept) one's feelings to oneself	die Gefühle für sich behalten
to keep up with sb.	mit jmd. mithalten
to kneel (knelt, knelt)	knien
lack of direction	Orientierungslosigkeit
lane	*hier:* kleine ländliche Straße
laziness	Faulheit
lemon curd tart	Zitronentorte
to lie	lügen
lonely	einsam
Long time no see!	Lange nicht gesehen!
to look after sb./sth.	für jmd./etw. sorgen
to be lost	*hier:* sich verlaufen haben
lovely	schön
to be lucky	Glück haben
↯ to make a big deal out of sth.	eine große Sache aus etw. machen
to make (made, made) decisions	Entscheidungen treffen
to manage	regeln, leiten
maple leaf	Ahornblatt
to marry	heiraten
mat	(Fuß-)Matte

medic	Sanitäter
to meet (met, met) (sb.'s) expectations	Erwartungen erfüllen
moan	Stöhnen
Mountain Rescue Team	Bergrettung
moustache	Schnurrbart
muddy	schlammig
mug	Becher
to mutter	murmeln
nasty	gemein, fies
nine-to-five job	Bürojob (mit geregelter Arbeitszeit)
to nod	nicken
noisy	laut
obese	fettleibig
obvious	offensichtlich
of course	natürlich, gewiss
Old Staff Association	Verband ehem. Mitarbeiter
on one's own	allein
on time	pünktlich, rechtzeitig
ϟ **Only joking!**	Nur ein Scherz!
open-neck (shirt)	offenes Hemd
open-plan office	Großraumbüro
opportunity	Gelegenheit
to order about	herumkommandieren
to pace	auf- und abgehen
painful	schmerzhaft
to pass	*hier:* vorübergehen
patch	Fleck, Stelle
path	Weg, Pfad
patient	geduldig
perhaps	vielleicht
permission	Erlaubnis
pill	Tablette
plate	Teller
to play a trick on sb.	jmd. einen Streich spielen
plum	Pflaume
powerful	kräftig
to practice	üben
to pretend	etw. vorgeben, vortäuschen
priceless	unbezahlbar
printing company	Druckerei
probably	wahrscheinlich
to promise	versprechen
proud	stolz
queue	(Warte-)Schlange

to raise one's eyebrows	die Stirn runzeln
rare	*hier:* blutig
relative	Verwandte/r
relieved	erleichtert
to remember	sich erinnern
to remind sb. to do sth.	jmd. daran erinnern, etw. zu tun
to rent	mieten
to replace sb.	jmd. ersetzen
to rescue	retten
responsibilities *pl*	*hier:* Verpflichtungen
retired	in Rente
rock	Felsen
rope	Seil
rotor blades *pl*	Rotorblätter
run	*hier:* Abfahrt, Piste
ϟ **to sack sb.**	jmd. feuern
saucer	Untertasse
to save up	(an)sparen
to scare	erschrecken
to be scared of heights	Höhenangst haben
to secure	*hier:* fixieren
to seem	scheinen, wirken
selfish	selbstsüchtig, egoistisch
to send (sent, sent) shivers up and down sb.'s spine	jdm. einen Schauder über den Rücken jagen
sense of humour	Sinn für Humor
serious	ernst(haft)
several	einige
to shake (shook, shaken) sb. out of sth.	*hier:* jmd. wachrütteln
to shake (shook, shaken)	beben, zittern
ϟ **shipshape**	tipptopp
to show off	angeben
to shuffle	schlurfen
shy(ly)	schüchtern
to be sick of sth.	etw. satt haben
to sigh	seufzen
sink	Spülbecken
to sit (sat, sat) up straight	aufrecht sitzen
ski goggles *pl*	Skibrille
ski lodge	Skihütte
skinny	dürr, mager
to slam on the brakes	eine Vollbremsung machen
to slam	*hier:* knallen
to slide	rutschen

smell	*hier:* Duft
to sniff	*hier:* schnüffeln
to snort	schnauben, prusten
snow-covered	mit Schnee bedeckt
snowplough position	im Pflug
sparkling	glitzernd, funkelnd
speechless	sprachlos
to speed up	schneller werden, beschleunigen
steep	steil
stool	Hocker
straight ahead	geradeaus
strange	merkwürdig, seltsam
stranger	Fremde/r
stream	Fluss, Bach
stretcher	Tragbahre
to stroke	streicheln
study	*hier:* Arbeitszimmer
successful	erfolgreich
suddenly	plötzlich
suffocating	erstickend
surprise visitor	Überraschungsbesuch
surprised	überrascht
to survive	überleben
sweetly	süß
to take turns	sich abwechseln
to tap	klopfen, tippen
tasty	schmackhaft, lecker
teaspoon	Teelöffel
ϟ **Thank goodness!**	Gott sei Dank!
the suburbs *pl*	Vorort, Stadtrand
The way to a man's heart is through his stomach.	Liebe geht durch den Magen.
threat	Bedrohung, Gefahr
tie	Krawatte
tightly	fest
ϟ **Till death us do part**	Bis dass der Tod uns scheidet
tin	*hier:* Dose
towel	Handtuch
to tuck	stecken, einklemmen
to twinkle	zwinkern, funkeln
to twitch	zucken
uncomfortable	unwohl
unfortunate	unglücklich
unlikely	unwahrscheinlich

to untie	losbinden
upset	aufgebracht, verärgert
usually	normalerweise
valley	Tal
vehicle	Fahrzeug
to wag (one's tail)	(mit dem Schwanz) wedeln
waiter	Bedienung
wardrobe	Kleiderschrank
waste of time	Zeitverschwendung
wastepaper bin	Papierkorb
wedding	Hochzeit
weird	seltsam, sonderbar
to whimper	wimmern, winseln
to whisper	flüstern
ϟ to whizz down the slopes	die Pisten heruntersausen
whole	ganz, gesamt
wife	Ehefrau
without batting an eyelid	ohne mit der Wimper zu zucken
to wonder	sich fragen
woolly	aus Wolle
to work magic	zaubern
to work	*hier:* funktionieren
to work out	*hier:* etw. herausfinden
worried	besorgt
to worry	sich Sorgen machen
to yell	brüllen

List of Exercises

COMPACT LERNKRIMI

Spannend Sprachen lernen

Kriminell gut

So bunt war Sprachenlernen noch nie!

- 3 spannende Comics für Anfänger ›
- landestypische Settings, actionreiche Szenen und authentische Sprache ›
- textbezogene Übungen nach jeder Geschichte ›
- Vokabelangaben auf jeder Seite ›
- Infokästen zu Sprache und Grammatik ›

ISBN 978-3-8174-1655-4

ISBN 978-3-8174-1856-5

Lernlektüre für geübte Anfänger

- ‹ 3 spannende Kurzkrimis
- ‹ über 50 textbezogene Übungen
- ‹ Vokabelangaben auf jeder Seite
- ‹ Infokästen zu Sprache und Grammatik
- ‹ von muttersprachlichen Autoren verfasst

www.lernkrimi.de | www.compactverlag.de